Core Knowledge Language Arts®

Domain 1
Fairy Tales and Tall Tales

Domain 2
Early Asian Civilizations

Domain 3
The Ancient Greek Civilization

Domain 4
Greek Myths

Domain 5
The War of 1812

Domain 6
Cycles in Nature

Domains 1 - 6
Tell it Again!™ Workbook

Listening & Learning™ Strand
GRADE 2

Amplify learning.

Core Knowledge®

Core Knowledge Language Arts®

Domain 1: Fairy Tales and Tall Tales
Tell It Again!™ Workbook

Listening & Learning™ Strand
GRADE 2

Amplify learning.

Core Knowledge®

Name _____

Title

Character(s)	Setting(s)

Plot

Beginning

Middle

End

Dear Family Member,

Today, your child heard the fairy tale "The Fisherman and His Wife," a story about a man who catches a magic fish that grants the fisherman's wife several wishes. In the coming days your child will hear two more fairy tales: "The Emperor's New Clothes" and "Beauty and the Beast." Below are some suggestions for activities that you may do at home to reinforce what your child is learning about fairy tales.

1. "The Fisherman and His Wife"

Have your child share what s/he remembers about the fairy tale "The Fisherman and His Wife." (A fisherman catches a flounder in the sea; the flounder tells the man he is actually an enchanted prince who has been turned into a flounder; the fisherman throws the flounder back; the fisherman's wife asks why he didn't first ask the flounder for a wish and sends him back to ask for several wishes; finally, the wife asks for too many things and the fish leaves them with what they had at the beginning of the story.) As your child shares what s/he remembers, fill in any gaps in the plot, and ask your child if s/he thinks there is a lesson to be learned from this fairy tale.

2. Draw and Write

Have your child draw and write a scene from any of the fairy tales s/he has heard ("The Fisherman and His Wife," "The Emperor's New Clothes," and "Beauty and the Beast"). Then have him/her share his/her drawing and writing with you. Ask questions to keep your child using the vocabulary learned at school.

3. "The Emperor's New Clothes"

Ask your child to retell the fairy tale "The Emperor's New Clothes." (An emperor finds great pleasure in dressing in different outfits; a strange weaver and tailor arrive and tell him they can make magical clothes, clothes only clever people can see; the emperor believes their story and hires them; everyone lies and says they can see the clothes in order to appear clever; a child finally states the truth.) Ask your child what they liked most about this fairy tale and if they think there is a lesson to be learned from this story.

4. Sayings and Phrases: Better Late Than Never

Your child will learn the saying "better late than never" in relation to the fairy tale "Beauty and the Beast." Ask your child how this saying relates to the fairy tale. (When Beauty decides to stay in the palace of the beast, she asks the beast to grant her one request: to say good-bye to her family. The beast grants her this request, but makes her promise to return before the full moon. Beauty doesn't return when promised, but does return to the palace just in time to save the beast's life.) Talk with your child about other situations where one might use the saying "better late than never."

5. Words to Use

Below is a list of some of the words that your child will be using and learning about. Try to use these words as they come up in everyday speech with your child.

- *enchanted*—The fisherman caught an enchanted fish that was able to grant him wishes.

- *admired*—The emperor admired himself in the mirror as he tried on his new clothes.

- *fearsome*—Beauty was terrified when she first laid eyes on the fearsome beast.

- *curious*—The beast told Beauty of all the curious events in the palace and how he was changed from a prince to a beast.

6. Read Aloud Each Day

It is very important that you read with your child every day. There should be time to read to your child and also time to listen to your child read to you. I have attached a list of recommended trade books related to fairy tales that may be found at the library.

Be sure to let your child know how much you enjoy hearing about what s/he has learned at school.

Recommended Trade Books for Fairy Tales and Tall Tales

Trade Book List

Original Anthologies

Note: These are large anthologies of the original fairy tales to show students the volume of the work of the Brothers Grimm.

1. *The Annotated Brothers Grimm (Bicentennial Edition)*, by Jacob Grimm and Wilhelm Grimm (W.W. Norton and Co., 2012) ISBN 978-3836526722

2. *The Fairy Tales of the Brothers Grimm*, by Jacob Grimm and Wilhelm Grimm (Taschen, 2011) ISBN 978-3836526722

3. *Grimm's Fairy Tales*, by Jacob Grimm and Wilhelm Grimm (CreateSpace Independent Publishing, 2012) ISBN 978-1480270251

Fairy Tales

4. *Beauty and the Beast,* retold and illustrated by Jan Brett (Sandpiper, 1990) ISBN 978-0395557020

5. *Beauty and the Beast,* by Max Eilenberg and illustrated by Angela Barrett (Candlewick, 2006) ISBN 978-0763631604

6. *Beauty and the Beast,* illustrated by Jess Stockham (Child's Play International, Ltd., 2008) ISBN 978-1846431142

7. *Beauty and the Beast,* retold by Louie Stowell and illustrated by Victor Tavares (Usborne Publishing Ltd., 2007) ISBN 978-0794518554

8. *The Emperor's New Clothes: A Tale Set in China,* by Demi (Margaret K. McElderry Books, 2000) ISBN 978-0689830686

9. *The Emperor's New Clothes,* by Hans Christian Andersen and illustrated by Virginia Lee Burton (Sandpiper, 2004) ISBN 978-0618344208

10. *The Emperor's New Clothes,* by Alison Edgson (Childs Play, 2007) ISBN 978-1846430206

11. *The Fisherman and His Wife,* by the Brothers Grimm and illustrated by John Howe (Creative Editions, 2001) ISBN 978-1568461403

12. *The Fisherman and His Wife,* retold and illustrated by Rachel Isadora (Putnam, 2008) ISBN 978-0399247712

13. *Liang and the Magic Paintbrush,* by Demi (Henry Holt and Co., 1988) ISBN 978-0805008012

14. *The Magic Fish,* by Freya Littledale and illustrated by Winslow Pinney Pels (Scholastic Inc., 1992) ISBN 978-0590411004

15. *A Tale of Two Parrots,* by Rashin Kheiriyeh (Enchanted Lion Books, 2013) ISBN 978-1592701308

Tall Tales

16. *Ain't Nothing But a Man: My Quest to Find John Henry,* by Scott Reynolds Nelson (National Geographic Children's Books, 2007) ISBN 978-1426300004

17. *American Tall Tales,* by Mary Pope Osborne and illustrated by Michael McCurdy (Knopf Books for Young Readers, 1991) ISBN 978-0679800897

18. *The Blind Men and the Elephant,* retold by Karen Backstein and illustrated by Annie Mitra (Scholastic Inc., 1992) ISBN 978-0590907392

19. *The Bunyans,* by Audrey Wood and illustrated by David Shannon (Scholastic Inc., 2006) ISBN 978-0439812146

20. *Casey Jones,* adapted by Stephen Krensky and illustrated by Mark Schroder (First Avenue Editions, 2007) ISBN 978-0822564768

21. *Calamity Jane,* adapted by Stephen Krensky and illustrated by Lisa Carlson (First Avenue Editions, 2007) ISBN 978-0822564805

22. *The Cu Bird,* by Marjorie Herrmann (McGraw-Hill, 1997) ISBN 978-0844271637

23. *The Enchanted Moccasins and Other Native American Legends,* by Henry R. Schoolcraft (Dover Publications, Inc., 2007) ISBN 978-0486460147

24. *John Henry: An American Legend,* by Ezra Jack Keats (Dragonfly Books, 1987) ISBN 978-0394890524

25. *John Henry,* by Julius Lester and illustrated by Jerry Pinkney (Puffin Books, 1999) ISBN 978-0140566222

26. *John Henry,* by Stephen Krensky and illustrated by Mark Oldroyd (Lerner, 2007) ISBN 978-0822564775

27. *Luba and the Wren,* by Patricia Polacco (Puffin Books, 2002) ISBN 978-0698119222

28. *Mike Fink,* adapted by Stephen Krensky and illustrated by Jeni Reeves (First Avenue Editions, 2007) ISBN 978-0822564782

29. *Mike Fink,* retold and illustrated by Steven Kellogg (HarperCollins, 1998) ISBN 978-0688135775

30. *Paul Bunyan,* retold and illustrated by Steven Kellogg (HarperCollins, 1985) ISBN 978-0688058005

31. *Paul Bunyan vs. Hals Halson: The Giant Lumberjack Challenge,* by Teresa Bateman and illustrated by C.B. Canga (Albert Whitman & Company, 2011) ISBN 978-0807563670

32. *Pecos Bill,* by Eric Blair and illustrated by Micah Chambers-Goldberg (Picture Window Books, 2013) ISBN 978-1479518609

33. *Pecos Bill,* retold and illustrated by Steven Kellogg (HarperCollins, 1992) ISBN 978-0688099244

34. *Sally Ann Thunder Ann Whirlwind Crockett,* retold and illustrated by Steven Kellogg (HarperCollins, 1995) ISBN 978-0688140427

35. *Swamp Angel,* by Anne Isaacs and illustrated by Paul O. Zelinsky (Puffin, 2000) ISBN 978-0140559088

36. *Totem Tale,* by Deb Vanasse and illustrated by Erik Brooks (Sasquatch Books, 2006) ISBN 978-1570614392

Websites

Student Resource

1. "Make a Story" Game
   http://pbskids.org/electriccompany/#/Games/Whats

Family Resources

2. John Henry: The Steel Driving Man
   http://www.ibiblio.org/john_henry/index.html

3. Present at the Creation: John Henry
   http://www.npr.org/programs/morning/features/patc/johnhenry

4. The Elements of a Fairy Tale
   http://www.surfturk.com/mythology/fairytaleelements.html

5. Origins of Paul Bunyan Story
   http://www.wisconsinhistory.org/topics/bunyan

6. The True Story of John Henry
   http://www.wvculture.org/history/africanamericans/henryjohn02.htm

Audio with video

7. "The Ballad of John Henry," by Harry Belafonte
   http://youtu.be/g6vcvYJCkic

8. "Casey Jones," by Johnny Cash
   http://youtu.be/mJCiPl-V6h8

Name _____

1. _____, the merchant went to see the cargo ship, hoping to restore his fortune.

   _____, the merchant lost his fortune, and his family became penniless.

2. _____, the merchant was riding his horse in a snowstorm.

   _____, the merchant found a castle where he could wait out the storm.

3. _____, the merchant picked a rose for Beauty.

   _____, the merchant found himself in a magical garden.

Name _____

Directions: Listen to each sentence read by the teacher. If the sentence is true, circle the smiling face. If the sentence is false, circle the frowning face.

1. ☺   ☹

2. ☺   ☹

3. ☺   ☹

4. ☺   ☹

5. ☺   ☹

6. ☺   ☹

7. ☺   ☹

8. ☺   ☹

9. ☺   ☹

Name _____

Directions: Fill in the chart with examples from each tall tale.

	Paul Bunyan	John Henry	Pecos Bil	Casey Jones
Amazing Childhood				
Creations/ Inventions				
Amazing Adventures				
Humor				
Exaggerations				

Dear Family Member,

Today, your child heard the tall tale "Paul Bunyan," a story about a fictional logger on the American frontier. Over the next few days, your child will hear three more tall tales about other larger-than-life characters on the American frontier—Pecos Bill, John Henry, and Casey Jones. Each tall tale will expose your child to the use of exaggeration. Below are some suggestions for activities that you may do at home to reinforce what your child is learning about tall tales.

1. Telling a Tall Tale

Ask your child what elements make a tall tale. (larger-than-life characters; exaggerations; amazing childhoods; unbelievable adventures; inventions of things in nature; humor) Ask your child to retell a tall tale. Then create your own tall tale with your child, asking him/her what kinds of characters and settings you will need. Ask him/her to provide ideas for your larger-than-life character's adventures.

2. Exaggerations

Have your child share some of the exaggerations s/he has heard from the tall tales. (Paul Bunyon straightened the Mississippi River and dug the Grand Canyon; Casey Jones drove a train and was known for always being on time; Pecos Bill rode a mountain lion and squeezed the meanness out of a rattlesnake; John Henry was born with a hammer in his hand and could swing a ten-pound hammer all day without getting tired.) Share with your child any literary exaggerations you know of.

3. Draw and Write

Have your child draw and write about what s/he has learned about any of the tall tale characters—Paul Bunyan, Pecos Bill, John Henry, or Casey Jones—and then have him/her share his/her drawing and writing with you. Ask questions to keep your child using the vocabulary learned at school.

4. Song: The Ballad of John Henry

Find a recording of "The Ballad of John Henry" from the public library or on the internet, and listen to it with your child. As you listen, have your child explain the tall tale of John Henry in his or her own words.

5. Words to Use

Below is a list of some of the words that your child will be using and learning about. Try to use these words as they come up in everyday speech with your child.

- *legendary*—Paul Bunyan was a legendary figure among real lumbermen on the frontier.

- *feat*—Tall tale characters always have adventures where they accomplish one amazing feat after another.

- *admiration*—Pecos Bill had a great deal of admiration for his horse, Lightning.

- *tame*—Tall tale characters rarely lead tame and unexciting lives.

6. Read Aloud Each Day

It is very important that you read with your child every day. There should be time to read to your child and also time to listen to your child read to you. I have attached a list of recommended trade books related to tall tales that may be found at the library.

Be sure to let your child know how much you enjoy hearing about what s/he has learned at school.

Name _____

Directions: Listen as your teacher reads each sentence. Write fact if the sentence states a fact. Write tall tale if the sentence is about something that could only happen in a tall tale.

1. _____ The Pecos River is in Texas.

2. _____ The coyote took Bill home to her den.

3. _____ Pecos Bill lassoed a tornado.

4. _____ Cyclones are real storms with very strong winds.

5. _____ Cowboys take care of cattle.

6. _____ A rattlesnake can be used as a lasso.

7. _____ A coyote looks like a small wolf.

Name _____

1. 🙂 ☹️

2. 🙂 ☹️

3. 🙂 ☹️

4. 🙂 ☹️

5. 🙂 ☹️

6. 🙂 ☹️

7. 🙂 ☹️

8. 🙂 ☹️

9. 🙂 ☹️

10. 🙂 ☹️

Directions: Listen to your teacher's instructions.

11.

12.

13.

14.

15.

Name _____

© 2013 Core Knowledge Foundation

Directions: Listen to each sentence read by the teacher. If the sentence is true, circle the smiling face. If the sentence is false, circle the frowning face.

1.   😊   ☹

2.   😊   ☹

3.   😊   ☹

4.   😊   ☹

5.   😊   ☹

6.   😊   ☹

7.   😊   ☹

8.   😊   ☹

9.   😊   ☹

Fairy Tales and Tall Tales

Name _____

Directions: Listen as your teacher reads each question, and think about the answer. Write words, phrases, or a sentence that come to mind when you hear each question.

1. Who was your favorite fairy tale character? Why?

    _____

    _____

    _____

2. Identify two exaggerations from any of the tall tales you heard. Make sure to also identify the character in each exaggeration.

    _____

    _____

    _____

3. What was your favorite fairy tale or tall tale setting? Why?

    _____

    _____

    _____

CORE KNOWLEDGE LANGUAGE ARTS

SERIES EDITOR-IN-CHIEF
E. D. Hirsch, Jr.

PRESIDENT
Linda Bevilacqua

EDITORIAL STAFF
Carolyn Gosse, Senior Editor - Preschool
Khara Turnbull, Materials Development Manager
Michelle L. Warner, Senior Editor - Listening & Learning

Mick Anderson
Robin Blackshire
Maggie Buchanan
Paula Coyner
Sue Fulton
Sara Hunt
Erin Kist
Robin Luecke
Rosie McCormick
Cynthia Peng
Liz Pettit
Ellen Sadler
Deborah Samley
Diane Auger Smith
Sarah Zelinke

DESIGN AND GRAPHICS STAFF
Scott Ritchie, Creative Director

Kim Berrall
Michael Donegan
Liza Greene
Matt Leech
Bridget Moriarty
Lauren Pack

CONSULTING PROJECT MANAGEMENT SERVICES
ScribeConcepts.com

ADDITIONAL CONSULTING SERVICES
Ang Blanchette
Dorrit Green
Carolyn Pinkerton

ACKNOWLEDGMENTS

These materials are the result of the work, advice, and encouragement of numerous individuals over many years. Some of those singled out here already know the depth of our gratitude; others may be surprised to find themselves thanked publicly for help they gave quietly and generously for the sake of the enterprise alone. To helpers named and unnamed we are deeply grateful.

CONTRIBUTORS TO EARLIER VERSIONS OF THESE MATERIALS
Susan B. Albaugh, Kazuko Ashizawa, Nancy Braier, Kathryn M. Cummings, Michelle De Groot, Diana Espinal, Mary E. Forbes, Michael L. Ford, Ted Hirsch, Danielle Knecht, James K. Lee, Diane Henry Leipzig, Martha G. Mack, Liana Mahoney, Isabel McLean, Steve Morrison, Juliane K. Munson, Elizabeth B. Rasmussen, Laura Tortorelli, Rachael L. Shaw, Sivan B. Sherman, Miriam E. Vidaver, Catherine S. Whittington, Jeannette A. Williams

We would like to extend special recognition to Program Directors Matthew Davis and Souzanne Wright who were instrumental to the early development of this program.

SCHOOLS
We are truly grateful to the teachers, students, and administrators of the following schools for their willingness to field test these materials and for their invaluable advice: Capitol View Elementary, Challenge Foundation Academy (IN), Community Academy Public Charter School, Lake Lure Classical Academy, Lepanto Elementary School, New Holland Core Knowledge Academy, Paramount School of Excellence, Pioneer Challenge Foundation Academy, New York City PS 26R (The Carteret School), PS 30X (Wilton School), PS 50X (Clara Barton School), PS 96Q, PS 102X (Joseph O. Loretan), PS 104Q (The Bays Water), PS 214K (Michael Friedsam), PS 223Q (Lyndon B. Johnson School), PS 308K (Clara Cardwell), PS 333Q (Goldie Maple Academy), Sequoyah Elementary School, South Shore Charter Public School, Spartanburg Charter School, Steed Elementary School, Thomas Jefferson Classical Academy, Three Oaks Elementary, West Manor Elementary.

And a special thanks to the CKLA Pilot Coordinators Anita Henderson, Yasmin Lugo-Hernandez, and Susan Smith, whose suggestions and day-to-day support to teachers using these materials in their classrooms was critical.

Core Knowledge Language Arts®

Domain 2: Early Asian Civilizations
Tell It Again!™ Workbook

Listening & Learning™ Strand
GRADE 2

Amplify learning.

Core Knowledge®

Name _____

Lesson 1: Label the continent of Asia on the title line above the map. Color in brown the border around the area formed by the present-day countries of India and Pakistan; label this area "ancient India." Color in brown the caret marks showing the mountains in ancient India; label these mountains "Himalayas." Label and color the Indus River in blue. Color the dot that represents the city of Mohenjo-daro next to the Indus River in red.

Lesson 3: Label and color the Ganges River in blue.

Lesson 8: Color in brown the border of China; label this area "China." Color in brown the caret marks showing the mountains in China; label these mountains "Bayankala Mountains." Label and color the Yellow River in yellow and the Yangtze River in blue. Add several dots in red around these rivers to represent cities that formed.

Title _____

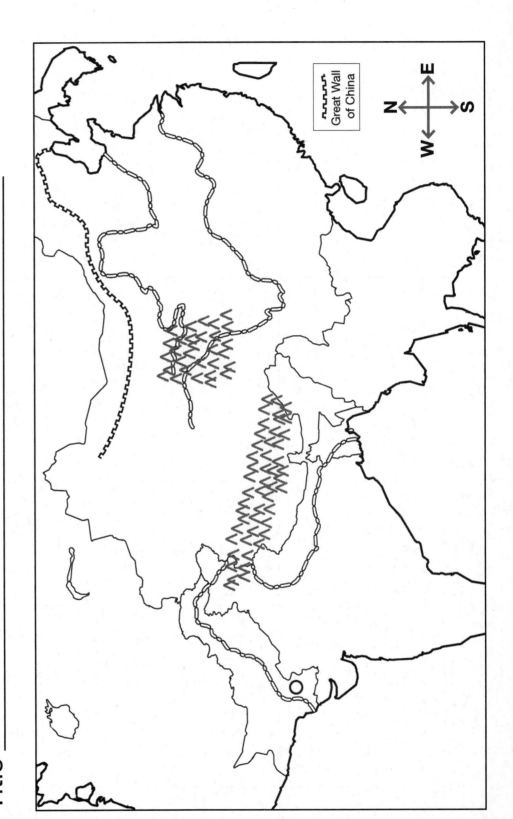

Dear Family Member,

Today, your child heard a read-aloud about the Indus River and the civilization that began in a nearby valley. Over the next several days, your child will learn more about life in early Asia, specifically ancient India. Your child will hear more about the Indus River Valley civilization as well as the civilization that began around the Ganges River. S/he will learn about some key features of civilizations, hear some folktales from early India, and will also learn about Hinduism and Buddhism, two religions that began in early India.

The Core Knowledge Language Arts program introduces students at various grade levels to the major world religions as part of their study of world history. The intent is to provide the vocabulary and context for understanding the many ways that the world religions have influenced ideas and events in history. The program's inclusion of world religions within the teaching of world history is comprehensive and balanced over the course of the elementary grades, presenting historical knowledge from around the world from ancient times to the present. It is important to understand that the religions your child will hear about in this domain—Hinduism and Buddhism—are not being singled out or presented in any way that suggests the merits or correctness of specific religious beliefs.

The read-alouds focus on teaching students very basic similarities and differences among religions, and fostering an understanding and respect for those similarities and differences. The historical events and ideas leading to the development of each religion are presented in a balanced and respectful manner. If students have questions about the truth or "rightness" of any beliefs or religions, we will encourage them to discuss their questions with you at home, by saying, "People of different faiths believe different things to be true. These are questions you may want to talk about with your family and the adults at home."

Please let us know if you have any questions.

Below are some suggestions for activities that you may do at home to reinforce what your child will learn about early Indian civilizations over the next few days.

1. Using a Map

Have your child locate the subcontinent of India on a world map. Remind your child that during the time period that we will call ancient India, present-day India and Pakistan were one country. Have your child tell you about the two mighty rivers in India and Pakistan, the Indus and the Ganges, and their significance to the beginning of early Indian civilization. Have your child describe how the rivers flooded and what the floodwaters left behind when they receded.

2. Hinduism

Talk with your child about this religion, the third-largest in the world. Have your child share with you some of the basic facts s/he has learned about Hinduism: Hindus worship many gods and goddesses; the three most important are Brahma, Vishnu, and Shiva; the Ganges River is sacred to Hindus; Hindus celebrate a festival called Diwali.

3. Buddhism

Talk with your child about this religion, the fourth-largest in the world. Have your child share with you some of the basic facts s/he has learned about Buddhism: Buddhism was started by Siddhartha Gautama, known by his followers as "the Buddha"; it is said that the Buddha achieved enlightenment and understood how to end suffering; Buddhists believe that suffering and unhappiness end when desires end.

4. Words to Use

Below is a list of some of the words that your child will be learning about and using. Try to use these words as they come up in everyday speech with your child.

- *fertile*—The land around the Indus River is very fertile with nutrient-rich soil.

- *cultivate*—The rich soil in the Indus River Valley makes it easier for farmers to cultivate crops.

- *recede*—The people who live near the Indus River are happy when the flood waters recede.

- *custom*—It is the Hindu custom to light lamps and candles each year during Diwali, the Festival of Lights.

- *conquer*—The Buddha meditated for forty-eight days, thinking of a way to conquer suffering and end unhappiness.

5. Read-Aloud Each Day

It is very important that you read to your child each day. The local library has many books on early Asian civilizations, such as India and China, and a list of books and other resources relevant to this topic is attached to this letter.

Be sure to let your child know how much you enjoy hearing about what s/he has learned at school.

Recommended Trade Books for Early Asian Civilizations

Trade Book List

Ancient India

1. *Ancient India,* edited by E.D. Hirsch, Jr. (Pearson Learning, 2002) ISBN 978-0769050140

2. *Diwali (Celebrations in My World),* by Kate Torpie (Crabtree Publishing Company, 2009) ISBN 978-0778743002

3. *Dumpling Days,* by Grace Lin (Little, Brown Books for Young Readers, 2013) ISBN 978-0316125895

4. *Lighting a Lamp: A Diwali Story,* by Jonny Zucker (Barron's Educational Series, Inc., 2004) ISBN 978-0764126703

5. *The Monkey and the Crocodile,* by Paul Galdone (Clarion Books, 1997) ISBN 978-0899195247

6. *One Grain of Rice,* by Demi (Scholastic Press, 1997) ISBN 978-0590939980

7. *Seven Blind Mice,* by Ed Young (Puffin Books, 2002) ISBN 978-0698118959

Ancient China

8. *Ancient China,* edited by E.D. Hirsch, Jr. (Pearson Learning, 2002) ISBN 978-0769050133

9. *The Ballad of Mulan: English/Hmong,* by Song Nan Zhang (Pan Asian Publications, 1998) ISBN 978-1572270589

10. *Colors of China,* by Shannon Zemlicka (Lerner Publishing Group, 2001) ISBN 978-1575055633

11. *Day of the Dragon King (Magic Tree House, No. 14),* by Mary Pope Osborne (Random House Books for Young Readers, 1998) ISBN 978-0679890515

12. *Dragon of the Red Dawn (Magic Tree House, No. 37),* by Mary Pope Osborne (Random House Books for Young Readers, 2008) ISBN 978-0375837289

13. *The Dragon Prince: A Chinese Beauty & the Beast Tale,* by Laurence Yep and illustrated by Kam Mak (HarperCollins, 1997) ISBN 978-0064435185

14. *The Emperor and the Kite,* by Jane Yolen and illustrated by Ed Young (Puffin, 1998) ISBN 978-0698116443

15. *The Great Wall of China,* by Leonard Everett Fisher (Aladdin, 1995) ISBN 978-0689801785

16. *Greetings, Asia!,* by April Pulley Sayre (Millbrook Press, 2003) ISBN 978-0761319917

17. *Look What Came from China,* by Miles Harvey (Franklin Watts, 1999) ISBN 978-0531159361

18. *Ming Lo Moves the Mountain,* by Arnold Lobel (Greenwillow Books, 1993) ISBN 978-0688109950

19. *The Seven Chinese Brothers,* by Margaret Mahy and illustrated by Mou-Sien Tseng (Scholastic Inc., 1990) ISBN 978-0590420570

20. *The Silk Route: 7,000 Miles of History,* by John S. Major (HarperCollins, 1996) ISBN 978-0064434683

21. *The Year of the Dog,* by Grace Lin (Little, Brown and Company, 2007) ISBN 978-0316060028

Teacher Resource

22. *Moonbeams, Dumplings & Dragon Boats: A Treasury of Chinese Holiday Tales, Activities & Recipes,* by Nina Simonds, Leslie Swartz, & The Children's Museum, Boston and illustrated by Meilo So (Harcourt, Inc., 2002) ISBN 978-0152019839

Websites and Other Resources

Student Resources

1. Asian Stories, Games, and Art for Students
   http://kids.asiasociety.org

2. Geography for Kids: Asian countries
   http://www.ducksters.com/geography/asia.php

3. World Religions: Hinduism and Buddhism
   http://www.uri.org/kids/world_hind.htm

Family Resources

4. American Museum of Natural History: Asian Peoples
   http://www.amnh.org/exhibitions/permanent-exhibitions/
   human-origins-and-cultural-halls/gardner-d.-stout-hall-of-asian-peoples

5. Chinese New Year
   http://www.history.com/topics/chinese-new-year

6. Diwali
   http://kids.nationalgeographic.com/kids/stories/peopleplaces/diwali/

7. Great Wall of China
   http://www.kinabaloo.com/great_wall_photo_gallery.html

Name _____

Directions: Read the characteristics of civilizations in the top row. Fill in the empty columns and rows as you learn more about early Indian civilization and early Chinese civilization.

	Farming	Cities	Writing	Leaders	Religion
Early Indian Civilization					
Early Chinese Civilization					

Directions: Read the headers at the top and the characteristics in the left-hand column. Fill in the empty columns and rows as you learn more about Hinduism and Buddhism.

Characteristics	Hinduism	Buddhism
Number of gods		
Name of followers		
Name of holy text(s)		
Holy place		
Important figure(s)		
Interesting fact		

Directions: There were many examples of personification in today's read-aloud. If a character behaved like a person, write the name of the character and the action underneath the word Person. If the character did not behave like a person, write the name of the character and the action underneath the words Not a Person.

Personification	
Person	**Not a Person**

Name _____

Directions: Read the characteristics of the Early Indian civilization in the top row. Fill in the empty columns.

	Farming	Cities	Writing	Leaders	Religion
Early Indian Civilization					

Dear Family Member,

Your child has learned how early Asian civilizations came into existence and what life was like during this time period. Over the next several days, s/he will learn about early Chinese civilizations, Chinese inventions such as paper and silk, and the Chinese form of writing called calligraphy. Your child will also learn about the creation of the Great Wall of China and the teachings of the famous philosopher Confucius.

Below are some suggestions for activities that you may do at home to reinforce what your child is learning about early Asian civilizations over the next few days.

1. Using a Map

Have your child locate China on a world map. Have your child tell you about the two mighty rivers in China, the Yellow and the Yangtze, and their significance to the beginning of Chinese civilization. Have your child describe how the rivers flooded and what the floodwaters left behind.

2. Compare and Contrast

Have your child share what s/he knows about the importance of writing and the invention of paper by the Chinese. Have your child compare and contrast the different types of writing surfaces that were used by the Chinese before paper was invented. Have your child share with you why some writing surfaces were better than others and how experimenting with different materials resulted in a smoother surface like the one we are familiar with today.

3. Sayings and Phrases: Easier Said Than Done/Practice What You Preach

Your child will learn about two sayings and their meanings in relation to the Great Wall of China and Confucius. Have your child share with you how the saying "easier said than done" relates to the Great Wall of China, that is, it was easier to say that there needed to be a protective wall in northern China than to actually build one; and how "practice what you preach" relates to Confucius, a man who believed that people also learned by example. Talk with your child about the meanings of and the situations in which you can use these two sayings.

4. Draw and Write

Have your child draw and/or write about what s/he has learned so far about early Chinese civilization and then share the drawing with you. Ask questions to help your child use the vocabulary learned at school.

5. Words to Use

Below is a list of some of the words that your child has been learning about and using. Try to use these words as they come up in everyday speech with your child.

- *remarkable*—It is remarkable that the writing system used in China today is very much like the one developed in the Yellow River Valley over three thousand years ago.

- *trade*—During the 13th and 14th centuries, Europe and Asia engaged in trade with one another along The Silk Roads.

- *transport*—People, donkeys, and goats were all used to transport the materials needed to build the Great Wall of China.

- *example*—Confucius believed that one could learn from books and also from the example of others.

- *prosperous*—Chinese people prepare for a prosperous year ahead during the two-week Chinese New Year celebration, just like Hindus do during Diwali.

6. Read Aloud Each Day

It is very important that you read to your child each day. Please refer to the list of books and other resources sent home with the previous family letter, recommending resources related to early Asian civilizations.

Be sure to let your child know how much you enjoy hearing about what s/he has learned at school.

Name _____

Brainstorming

Step 1	Step 2

Step 3	Step 4

Directions: In the boxes provided, brainstorm the steps to get silk thread from silkworms.

Name _____

Directions: Use this paper for your writing. Remember to write complete sentences that begin with a capital letter and end with the correct punctuation.

_____

_____

_____

_____

_____

_____

_____

_____

_____

_____

_____

_____

_____

Directions: Think about what you have heard in the read-aloud, and then fill in the chart using words or sentences.

Somebody	
Wanted	
But	
So	
Then	

Name _____

Directions: Think about how these two individuals are similar and how they are different. Draw or write how they are alike in the overlapping part of the two circles. Draw or write how the Buddha is different from Confucius in the right-hand circle. Draw or write how Confucius is different from the Buddha in the left-hand circle.

Confucius

the Buddha

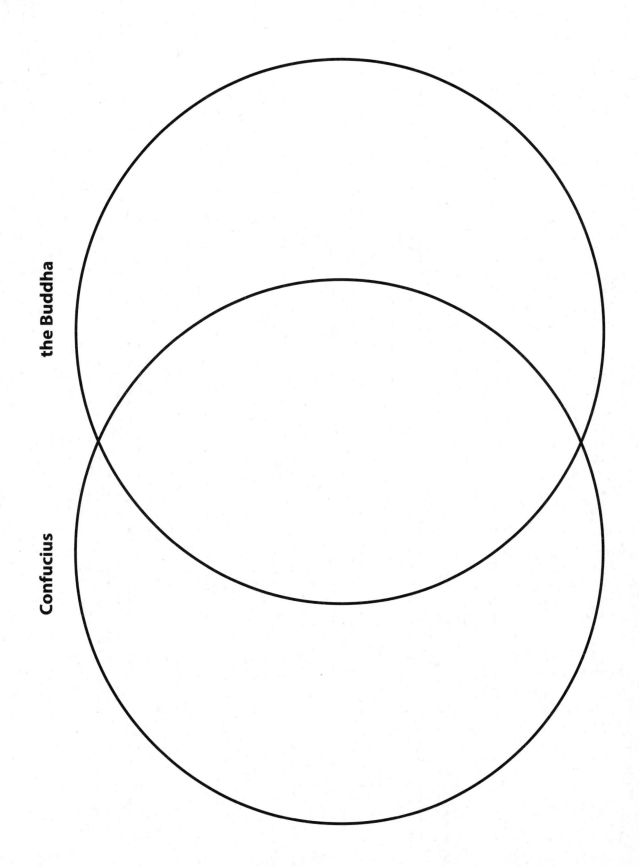

Name _____

Directions: Think about how these two celebrations are similar and how they are different. Draw or write how they are alike in the overlapping part of the two circles. Draw or write how Diwali is different from the Chinese New Year in the left-hand circle. Draw or write how the Chinese New Year is different from Diwali in the right-hand circle.

Chinese New Year

Diwali

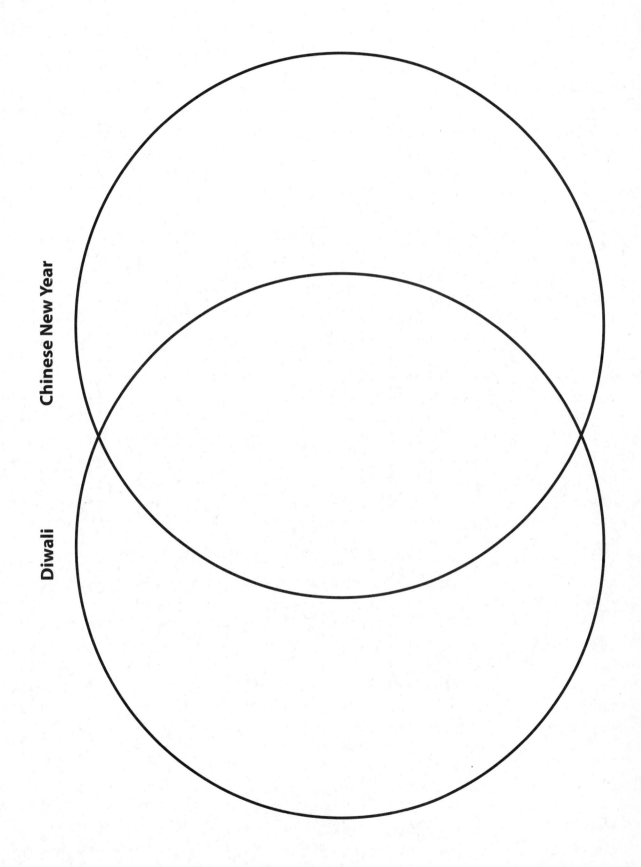

Name _____

1.

2.

3.

4.

5.

6.

7.

8.

9.

10.

Directions: Listen to your teacher's instructions.

Name _____

Directions: Title your map with the name of the continent, and then label the mountains, rivers, and countries you learned about in this domain. You may reference the word bank below to help you.

Title _____

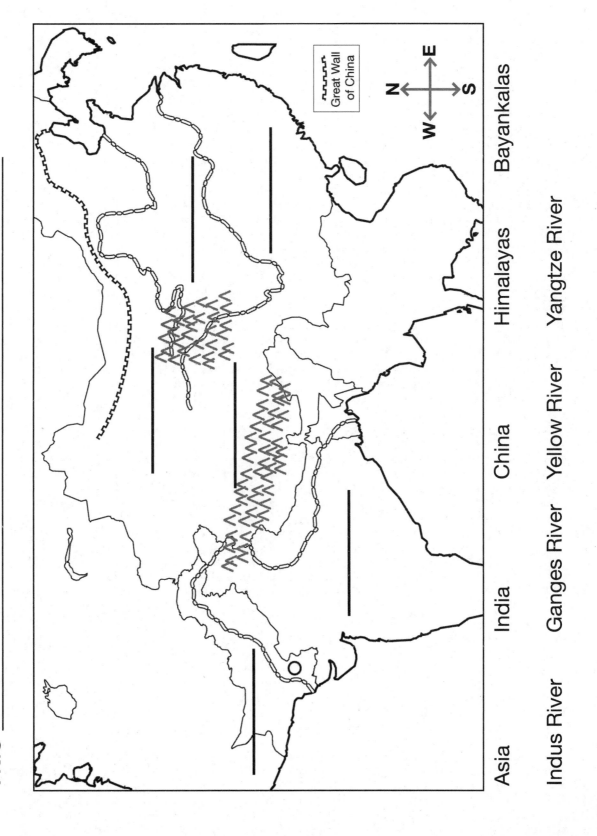

Great Wall of China

N
W — E
S

Asia   India   China   Himalayas   Bayankalas

Indus River   Ganges River   Yellow River   Yangtze River

Name _____

Directions: Listen to each sentence read by the teacher. Think about the answer for each question. Write at least one complete sentence to answer each question.

1.   Who was Confucius?

_____

_____

_____

_____

_____

2.   Describe either the Chinese New Year or Diwali.

_____

_____

_____

_____

_____

3. How were rivers important to the development of early Indian and early Chinese civilizations?

_____

_____

_____

_____

4. What is the most interesting thing you learned about Hinduism or Buddhism and why?

_____

_____

_____

_____

Name _____

Directions: Use this instructional master as a guide for copying the Chinese characters 1–12 when making your Chinese clock.

1	一
2	二
3	三
4	四
5	五
6	六
7	七
8	八
9	九
10	十
11	十一
12	十二

CORE KNOWLEDGE LANGUAGE ARTS

SERIES EDITOR-IN-CHIEF
E. D. Hirsch, Jr.

PRESIDENT
Linda Bevilacqua

EDITORIAL STAFF
Carolyn Gosse, Senior Editor - Preschool
Khara Turnbull, Materials Development Manager
Michelle L. Warner, Senior Editor - Listening & Learning

Mick Anderson
Robin Blackshire
Maggie Buchanan
Paula Coyner
Sue Fulton
Sara Hunt
Erin Kist
Robin Luecke
Rosie McCormick
Cynthia Peng
Liz Pettit
Ellen Sadler
Deborah Samley
Diane Auger Smith
Sarah Zelinke

DESIGN AND GRAPHICS STAFF
Scott Ritchie, Creative Director

Kim Berrall
Michael Donegan
Liza Greene
Matt Leech
Bridget Moriarty
Lauren Pack

CONSULTING PROJECT MANAGEMENT SERVICES
ScribeConcepts.com

ADDITIONAL CONSULTING SERVICES
Ang Blanchette
Dorrit Green
Carolyn Pinkerton

ACKNOWLEDGMENTS

These materials are the result of the work, advice, and encouragement of numerous individuals over many years. Some of those singled out here already know the depth of our gratitude; others may be surprised to find themselves thanked publicly for help they gave quietly and generously for the sake of the enterprise alone. To helpers named and unnamed we are deeply grateful.

CONTRIBUTORS TO EARLIER VERSIONS OF THESE MATERIALS
Susan B. Albaugh, Kazuko Ashizawa, Nancy Braier, Kathryn M. Cummings, Michelle De Groot, Diana Espinal, Mary E. Forbes, Michael L. Ford, Ted Hirsch, Danielle Knecht, James K. Lee, Diane Henry Leipzig, Martha G. Mack, Liana Mahoney, Isabel McLean, Steve Morrison, Juliane K. Munson, Elizabeth B. Rasmussen, Laura Tortorelli, Rachael L. Shaw, Sivan B. Sherman, Miriam E. Vidaver, Catherine S. Whittington, Jeannette A. Williams

We would like to extend special recognition to Program Directors Matthew Davis and Souzanne Wright who were instrumental to the early development of this program.

SCHOOLS
We are truly grateful to the teachers, students, and administrators of the following schools for their willingness to field test these materials and for their invaluable advice: Capitol View Elementary, Challenge Foundation Academy (IN), Community Academy Public Charter School, Lake Lure Classical Academy, Lepanto Elementary School, New Holland Core Knowledge Academy, Paramount School of Excellence, Pioneer Challenge Foundation Academy, New York City PS 26R (The Carteret School), PS 30X (Wilton School), PS 50X (Clara Barton School), PS 96Q, PS 102X (Joseph O. Loretan), PS 104Q (The Bays Water), PS 214K (Michael Friedsam), PS 223Q (Lyndon B. Johnson School), PS 308K (Clara Cardwell), PS 333Q (Goldie Maple Academy), Sequoyah Elementary School, South Shore Charter Public School, Spartanburg Charter School, Steed Elementary School, Thomas Jefferson Classical Academy, Three Oaks Elementary, West Manor Elementary.

And a special thanks to the CKLA Pilot Coordinators Anita Henderson, Yasmin Lugo-Hernandez, and Susan Smith, whose suggestions and day-to-day support to teachers using these materials in their classrooms was critical.

Domain 3:
The Ancient Greek Civilization
Tell It Again!™ Workbook

Listening & Learning™ Strand
GRADE 2

Amplify learning.

Core Knowledge®

Name _____

The Ancient Greek Civilizations Chart

Jobs	City-States

Leaders	Religion

The Ancient Greek Civilizations Chart

Contributions

Dear Family Member,

Over the next couple of weeks, your child will learn about the ancient Greek civilization, a group of people whose contributions can be seen in many areas of our lives today, specifically in our democratic government. Your child will be introduced to the geography and gods and goddesses of this civilization. S/he will also learn about the city-states of Sparta and Athens and the very first Olympic Games held in honor of Zeus.

Below are some suggestions for activities that you may do at home to reinforce what your child is learning about the ancient Greek civilization.

1. Draw and Write

Ask your child to draw and/or write about what s/he is learning about the ancient Greek civilization, such as the gods and goddesses who were believed to live on Mount Olympus or the first Olympic Games. Ask questions to help your child use the vocabulary learned at school.

2. Sayings and Phrases: Where There's a Will There's a Way

Your child will be learning the saying "Where there's a will there's a way." Talk with your child about its meaning. Share moments in your life when you or someone you know has accomplished something because of great determination or a strong will.

3. Words to Use

Below is a list of some of the words that your child will be learning about and using. Try to use these words as they come up in everyday speech with your child.

- *rugged*—Although the rugged terrain of ancient Greece made farming difficult, the olive tree was one hardy plant the Greeks were able to grow in abundance.

- *massive*—The ancient Greeks imagined that the god of the sea, Poseidon, was massive in size and strength, for they believed he could make the earth quake and the waves crash upon the shore.

- *grove*—The ancient Greeks believed that at the request of the goddess Athena, the goddess Demeter made each grove of olive trees grow strong for the Athenians.

- *sacred*—The city of Olympia was a sacred place; the ancient Greeks gathered there to honor the gods with games and worship.

- *self-discipline*—The people of Sparta were known for their self-discipline, for they spent their lives training for battle and did not allow themselves any luxuries.

4. Read Aloud Each Day

It is very important that you read with your child every day. Set aside time to read to your child and also time to listen to your child read to you. Attached is a list of recommended trade books related to *The Ancient Greek Civilization*. Many of these may be found at the library.

Be sure to let your child know how much you enjoy hearing what s/he has learned at school.

Recommended Resources for The Ancient Greek Civilization

Trade Books

1. *Ancient Greece,* edited by E. D. Hirsch, Jr. (Pearson Learning, 2002) ISBN 978-0769050164

2. *Ancient Greece (DK Eyewitness Books),* by Anne Pearson (DK Children, 2007) ISBN 978-0756630027

3. *Ancient Greece (True Books: Ancient Civilizations),* by Sandra Newman (Children's Press, 2010) ISBN 978-0531241073

4. *Ancient Greece (Cultural Atlas for Young People),* by Anton Powell (Chelsea House Publications, 2007) ISBN 978-0816068210

5. *Ancient Greece and the Olympics: A Nonfiction Companion to Hour of the Olympics,* by Mary Pope Osborne and Natalie Pope Boyce (Random House Books for Young Readers, 2004) ISBN 978-0375823787

6. *The Gods and Goddesses of Olympus,* by Aliki (HarperCollins, 1997) ISBN 978-0064461894

7. *The Greeks (Starting History),* by Sally Hewitt (Smart Apple Media, 2008) ISBN 978-1599200453

8. *Hour of the Olympics* (Magic Tree House, No. 16), by Mary Pope Osborne (Random House Books for Young Readers, 1998) ISBN 978-0679890621

9. *I Wonder Why Greeks Built Temples and Other Questions About Ancient Greece,* by Fiona Macdonald (Kingfisher Publications, 2012) ISBN 978-0753467053

10. *Life in a Greek Trading Port,* by Jane Shuter (Heinemann Library, 2005) ISBN 978-1403464514

11. *Life in Ancient Athens,* by Jane Shuter (Heinemann Library, 2005) ISBN 978-1403464507

12. *Tools of the Ancient Greeks: A Kid's Guide to the History & Science of Life in Ancient Greece,* by Kris Bordessa (Nomad Press, 2006) ISBN 978-0974934464

Websites and Other Resources

Student Resources

1. Ancient Greek Gods
    http://bit.ly/Z0qLRi

2. Birmingham Museum and Art Gallery for Kids: Ancient Greece
    http://bit.ly/VeuRlR

3. Metropolitan Museum of Art
    http://bit.ly/Wk46nP

4. Socrates, Plato, and Aristotle
    http://bit.ly/13qiNrS

Family Resources

5. Battle of Marathon
    http://bit.ly/XnCFGV

6. Sparta
    http://bit.ly/Y81eYx

7. The Parthenon
    http://bit.ly/ZEl2Tk

Name _____

Directions: Write the two topics you have chosen to compare/contrast on the blanks. Write how the two topics are similar in the overlapping part of the Venn diagram. Write how the topics are different in the circle for each topic.

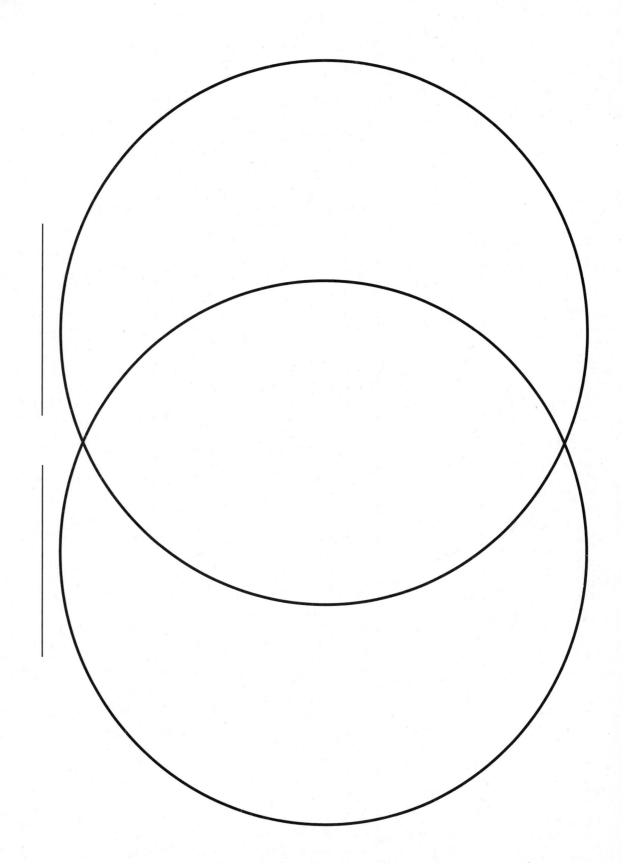

The Ancient Greek Civilizations   **7**

Directions: Think about what you heard in the read-aloud to fill in the chart using words or sentences.

Somebody	
Wanted	
But	
So	
Then	

Dear Family Member,

I hope your child is enjoying learning about the ancient Greek civilization. Over the next several days, s/he will learn more about the contributions of this civilization, as well as the significance of the Battles of Marathon and Thermopylae. S/he will also be introduced to the Greek philosophers Socrates, Plato, and Aristotle, and to the conqueror Alexander the Great. Your child will also write a narrative "You Were There" paragraph describing what his or her life might be like as an ancient Greek.

Below are some suggestions for activities that you may do at home to reinforce what your child is learning about the ancient Greek civilization.

1. Draw and Write

Have your child draw and/or write about what s/he is learning about the ancient Greek civilization, such as Pheidippides's marathon run or the Greek philosophers. Ask questions to help your child use the vocabulary learned at school.

2. Sayings and Phrases: Practice What You Preach

Your child will be learning the saying "practice what you preach." Talk with your child about its meaning. Share moments in your life when you or someone you know has lived his/her life in the same way that s/he has told others they should live.

3. Words to Use

Below is a list of some of the words that your child will learn about and use. Try to use these words as they come up in everyday speech with your child.

- *marathon*—The ancient Greeks honored Pheidippides for his twenty-six-mile marathon run.

- *channel*—Swimming through the cold waters of the English Channel has been a challenge for many long-distance swimmers.

- *philosopher*—Socrates was known as a famous Greek philosopher.

- *ambitious*—Alexander the Great was an ambitious leader who had a strong desire for success.

- *flung*—The Olympic champion flung his disc farther than anyone else.

4. Read Aloud Each Day

It is very important that you read with your child every day. Set aside time to read to your child and also time to listen to your child read to you. Use the recommended trade book list sent with the previous family letter.

Be sure to let your child know how much you enjoy hearing what s/he has learned at school.

Name _____

Directions: Choose a character who lived in ancient Greek times (Spartan boy, Athenian girl, seafarer from Crete, etc.). Write the character's name in the center oval. On the spokes of the oval, write everything that comes to mind about who your character is, where s/he lives, and what s/he experiences every day.

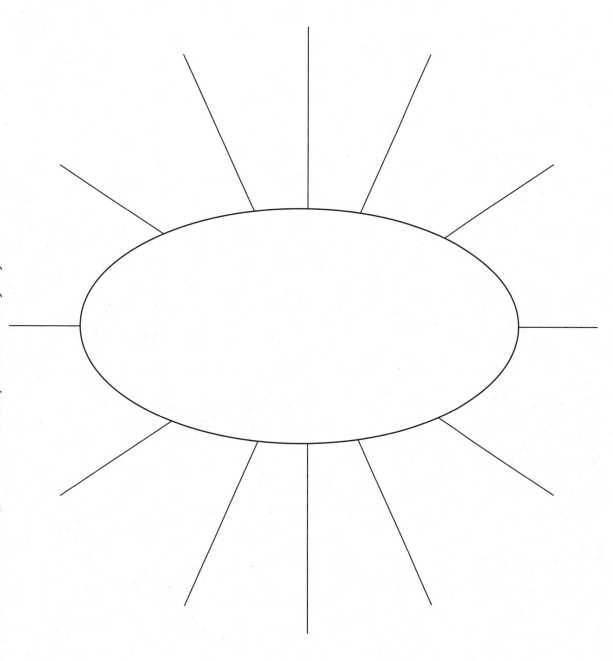

Name _____

Directions: Write the introductory sentence for your paragraph in the first rectangle. Write the three descriptive sentences in the second, third, and fourth rectangles. Write your concluding sentence in the fifth rectangle.

The Ancient Greek Civilizations

Name _____

Alexander the Great's Empire

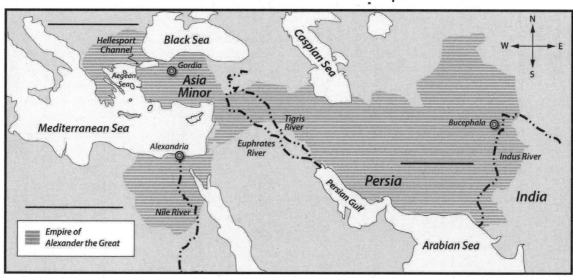

1. What does the shaded area stand for on the map?

    _____

    _____

2. Alexander's empire included parts of which continents?

    _____

    _____

3. Which area of land was larger: the area where the ancient Greek civilizations existed, or the area that Alexander the Great conquered?

    _____

    _____

    _____

Name _____

Directions: Listen to your teacher's directions about this checklist. Then look at your writing to see if you have ended each sentence with the correct punctuation, put commas between items in a list, and started each sentence with a capital letter. Your teacher will let you know if there are other things you should look for in your writing.

. ? !

, ,

The cat ran.

Directions: Write the two topics you have chosen to compare/contrast on the blanks. Write how the two topics are similar in the overlapping part of the Venn diagram. Write how the topics are different in the circle for each topic.

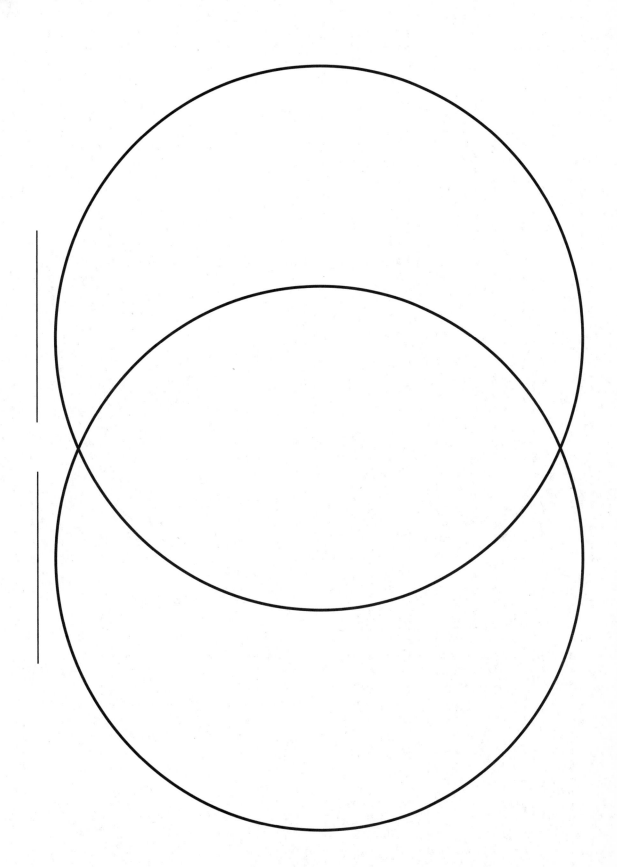

Directions: Listen to your teacher's instructions.

1.

2.

3.

4.

5.

6.

7.

8.

9.

10.

11.

12.

13.

14.

15.

Name _____

Directions: Listen to each sentence read by the teacher. Then listen to the three names in each row. Circle the name of the person the teacher has described.

1.   Athena   Zeus   Apollo

2.   Zeus   Hermes   Athena

3.   Aristotle   Alexander the
                        Great   Plato

4.   Socrates   Plato   Aristotle

Name _____

Directions: Listen to the sentence read by the teacher. Circle the smiling face if the sentence is true. Circle the frowning face if the sentence is false.

1. ☺ ☹

2. ☺ ☹

3. ☺ ☹

4. ☺ ☹

5. ☺ ☹

6. ☺ ☹

7. ☺ ☹

8. ☺ ☹

9. ☺ ☹

10. ☺ ☹

11.

Name _____

Directions: Listen to your teacher read each sentence. Think about the answer to the question. Write a few words, phrases, or sentences to answer each question or statement.

1. Choose one of the Greek gods or goddesses you have learned about, and write about a particular power or skill s/he was believed to possess.

_____

_____

_____

_____

_____

2. What are some contributions that the ancient Greeks gave to the rest of the world?

_____

_____

_____

_____

_____

3. If you could meet one of the people you learned about, whom would you choose? Why?

_____

_____

_____

_____

4. How were Sparta and Athens similar? How were they different?

_____

_____

_____

_____

5. What was the most interesting thing you learned about the ancient Greek civilizations?

_____

_____

_____

_____

Name _____

Title: _____

_____

_____

_____

_____

_____

_____

_____

_____

_____

_____

_____

_____

_____

_____

Directions: Use this paper for your summary. Remember to write in complete sentences that begin with a capital letter and end with the correct punctuation.

CORE KNOWLEDGE LANGUAGE ARTS

SERIES EDITOR-IN-CHIEF
E. D. Hirsch, Jr.

PRESIDENT
Linda Bevilacqua

EDITORIAL STAFF
Carolyn Gosse, Senior Editor - Preschool
Khara Turnbull, Materials Development Manager
Michelle L. Warner, Senior Editor - Listening & Learning

Mick Anderson
Robin Blackshire
Maggie Buchanan
Paula Coyner
Sue Fulton
Sara Hunt
Erin Kist
Robin Luecke
Rosie McCormick
Cynthia Peng
Liz Pettit
Ellen Sadler
Deborah Samley
Diane Auger Smith
Sarah Zelinke

DESIGN AND GRAPHICS STAFF
Scott Ritchie, Creative Director

Kim Berrall
Michael Donegan
Liza Greene
Matt Leech
Bridget Moriarty
Lauren Pack

CONSULTING PROJECT MANAGEMENT SERVICES
ScribeConcepts.com

ADDITIONAL CONSULTING SERVICES
Ang Blanchette
Dorrit Green
Carolyn Pinkerton

ACKNOWLEDGMENTS

These materials are the result of the work, advice, and encouragement of numerous individuals over many years. Some of those singled out here already know the depth of our gratitude; others may be surprised to find themselves thanked publicly for help they gave quietly and generously for the sake of the enterprise alone. To helpers named and unnamed we are deeply grateful.

CONTRIBUTORS TO EARLIER VERSIONS OF THESE MATERIALS

Susan B. Albaugh, Kazuko Ashizawa, Nancy Braier, Kathryn M. Cummings, Michelle De Groot, Diana Espinal, Mary E. Forbes, Michael L. Ford, Ted Hirsch, Danielle Knecht, James K. Lee, Diane Henry Leipzig, Martha G. Mack, Liana Mahoney, Isabel McLean, Steve Morrison, Juliane K. Munson, Elizabeth B. Rasmussen, Laura Tortorelli, Rachael L. Shaw, Sivan B. Sherman, Miriam E. Vidaver, Catherine S. Whittington, Jeannette A. Williams

We would like to extend special recognition to Program Directors Matthew Davis and Souzanne Wright who were instrumental to the early development of this program.

SCHOOLS

We are truly grateful to the teachers, students, and administrators of the following schools for their willingness to field test these materials and for their invaluable advice: Capitol View Elementary, Challenge Foundation Academy (IN), Community Academy Public Charter School, Lake Lure Classical Academy, Lepanto Elementary School, New Holland Core Knowledge Academy, Paramount School of Excellence, Pioneer Challenge Foundation Academy, New York City PS 26R (The Carteret School), PS 30X (Wilton School), PS 50X (Clara Barton School), PS 96Q, PS 102X (Joseph O. Loretan), PS 104Q (The Bays Water), PS 214K (Michael Friedsam), PS 223Q (Lyndon B. Johnson School), PS 308K (Clara Cardwell), PS 333Q (Goldie Maple Academy), Sequoyah Elementary School, South Shore Charter Public School, Spartanburg Charter School, Steed Elementary School, Thomas Jefferson Classical Academy, Three Oaks Elementary, West Manor Elementary.

And a special thanks to the CKLA Pilot Coordinators Anita Henderson, Yasmin Lugo-Hernandez, and Susan Smith, whose suggestions and day-to-day support to teachers using these materials in their classrooms was critical.

Core Knowledge Language Arts®

Domain 4: Greek Myths
Tell It Again!™ Workbook

Listening & Learning™ Strand
GRADE 2

Amplify learning.

Core Knowledge®

Name _____

Directions: Use this worksheet for your writing. Remember to write complete sentences that begin with a capital letter and end with the correct punctuation.

Title: _____

_____

_____

_____

_____

_____

_____

_____

_____

_____

_____

_____

_____

_____

_____

_____

Dear Family Member,

Today, your child heard a read-aloud about the twelve Greek gods and goddesses that the ancient Greeks believed lived on Mount Olympus. Over the next several days, your child will review that the ancient Greeks worshipped many gods and goddesses, and that the twelve on Mount Olympus were thought to be the most powerful. S/he will learn the definition of a myth (a fictional story, once thought to be true), and that myths try to explain occurrences in nature, teach moral stories, and entertain listeners. Your child will hear several well-known Greek myths including "Prometheus and Pandora," "Demeter and Persephone," and "Arachne the Weaver."

Below are some suggestions for activities that you may do at home to reinforce what your child is learning about Greek myths.

1. The Twelve Gods of Mount Olympus

Have your child share which twelve gods and goddesses the ancient Greeks thought lived on Mount Olympus and what these gods and goddesses were in charge of. (Zeus, Poseidon, Demeter, Hera, Hephaestus, Aphrodite, Athena, Ares, Apollo, Artemis, Hermes, Dionysus) As your child shares what they know about these twelve Greek gods and goddesses, share with them what you know, including any Greek gods and goddesses that they have not heard about.

2. Prometheus and Pandora

Have your child share what s/he learned about Prometheus. (His name means foresight; the ancient Greeks believed that he created humans; he stole fire to give to man; Zeus punished him.) Have your child share what s/he learned about Pandora. (The Greek gods made her with wonderful characteristics; they sent her to Earth with a box, which she was not supposed to open; she opened it and let out all the things that cause people pain and suffering.) Talk with your child about the saying, "Pandora's box" and in what situations one might use it.

3. Demeter and Persephone

Talk with your child about the myth of Demeter and Persephone. Have your child share which characters appeared in this myth and how this myth was a way for ancient Greeks to explain the changing seasons.

4. Sayings and Phrases: Cold Feet

Your child will learn the saying "cold feet" in relation to the Greek myth of Daedalus and Icarus. Before Daedalus and his son Icarus use their wax wings to try to escape from the prison tower, Daedalus hesitates with sudden fear. Talk with your child about other situations where one might use the saying "cold feet."

5. Words to Use

Below is a list of some of the words that your child will be learning about and using. Try to use these words as they come up in everyday speech with your child.

- myths—Many ancient peoples told myths, fictional stories thought to be true at the time, that tried to explain events in nature.

- mortal—All humans are mortal, which means that they are born and later die.

- immortal—Greek gods and goddesses were believed to be immortal, which means they never die.

6. Read-Aloud Each Day

It is very important that you read to your child each day. The local library has many books on Greek myths and ancient Greek civilization, and a list of books and other resources relevant to this topic is attached to this letter.

Be sure to let your child know how much you enjoy hearing about what s/he has learned at school.

Recommended Trade Books for Greek Myths

Trade Book List

1. *A Child's Introduction to Greek Mythology: The Stories of the Gods, Goddesses, Heroes, Monsters, and Other Mythical Creatures,* by Heather Alexander (Black Dog & Leventhal Publishers, 2011) ISBN 978-1579128678

2. *D'Aulaires' Book of Greek Myths,* by Ingri and Edgar Parin D'Aulaire (Delacorte Press, 1962) ISBN 978-0440406945

3. *Gifts from the Gods: Ancient Words and Wisdom from Greek and Roman Mythology,* by Lise Lunge-Larsen (Houghton Mifflin Books for Children, 2011) ISBN 978-0547152295

4. *The Gods and Goddesses of Olympus,* by Aliki (HarperCollins, 1997) ISBN 978-0064461894

5. *Greek Myths,* by Deborah Lock (DK Publishing, 2008) ISBN 978-0756640156

6. *Greek Myths,* by Marcia Williams (Candlewick, 2011) ISBN 978-0763653842

7. *King Midas: The Golden Touch,* by Demi (Margaret K. McElderry Books, 2002) ISBN 978-0689832970

8. *The McElderry Book of Greek Myths,* retold by Eric A. Kimmel (Margaret K. McElderry Books, 2008) ISBN 978-1416915348

9. *Mythological Creatures: A Classical Bestiary,* by Lynn Curlee (Atheneum Books for Young Readers, 2008) ISBN 978-1416914532

10. *Pandora,* by Robert Burleigh (Harcourt, Inc., 2002) ISBN 978-0152021788

11. *Pegasus,* by Marianna Mayer (Morrow Junior Books, 1998) ISBN 978-0688133825

Websites and Other Resources

Student Resources

1. Greek Coloring Pages
    http://www.coloring.ws/greek.htm

2. Myths Brainstorming Machine
    http://teacher.scholastic.com/writewit/mff/mythmachine.htm

Family Resources

3. Additional Greek Myths
    http://greece.mrdonn.org/myths.html

4. Greek Gods/Twelve Olympians
    http://greece.mrdonn.org/greekgods/mountolympus.html

5. Miscellaneous Activities for Greek Myths
    http://www.activityvillage.co.uk/ancient_greece_for_kids.htm

6. Mt. Olympus
    http://travel.nationalgeographic.com/travel/parks/olympus-greece/

Name _____

Directions: These six pictures show events from the myth "Prometheus and Pandora." Cut out the six pictures. Think about what is happening in each one. Put the pictures in order to show the sequence of events in the myth. Glue them in the correct order on a piece of paper.

Name _____

Name _____

Title: _____

_____

_____

_____

_____

_____

_____

_____

_____

_____

_____

_____

Name _____

Title: _____

Directions: Use this worksheet for your writing and drawing. Remember to write complete sentences that begin with a capital letter and end with the correct punctuation.

Name _____

Greek Myths

Title: _____

_____

_____

_____

_____

_____

_____

_____

_____

_____

_____

Title: _____

Directions: Use this worksheet for your writing and drawing. Remember to write complete sentences that begin with a capital letter and end with the correct punctuation.

_____

_____

_____

_____

_____

_____

_____

_____

_____

_____

Name _____

Directions: Listen to each pair of sentences as your teacher reads them. Write First on the blank before the sentence that happened first in the story, and write Then on the blank before the sentence that happens second in the story.

1. _____, Theseus defeats the Minotaur.

_____, Theseus meets his father.

2. _____, Theseus forgets to change the sails from black to white.

_____, King Aegeus falls into the sea.

3. _____, Theseus ties the gold thread around his body.

_____, King Minos's son dies in Athens.

4. _____, Daedalus creates the Labyrinth.

_____, Princess Ariadne asks Daedalus how to help Theseus escape from the Labyrinth.

Name _____

Title: _____

Directions: Use this worksheet for your writing and drawing. Remember to write complete sentences that begin with a capital letter and end with the correct punctuation.

_____

_____

_____

_____

_____

_____

_____

_____

_____

_____

Name _____

Directions: These five pictures show events from the myth "Demeter and Persephone." Cut out the five pictures. Think about what is happening in each one. Put the pictures in order to show the sequence of events in the myth. Glue them in the correct order on a piece of paper.

Name _____

Directions: Think about what you have heard in the read-aloud, and then fill in the chart using words or sentences.

Somebody	
Wanted	
But	
So	
Then	

Title: _____

Directions: Use this worksheet for your writing and drawing. Remember to write complete sentences that begin with a capital letter and end with the correct punctuation.

Name _____

Directions: Use this story map to describe the characters, settings, and plot of the story.

Title: _____

| Character(s) | Setting(s) |

Plot

Beginning

Middle

End

Name _____

Directions: Use this story map to brainstorm the characters, setting, and plot of your Greek myth.

Title: _____

Character(s)	Setting(s)

Plot

Beginning

Middle

End

Dear Family Member,

Today, your child heard a read-aloud about the most famous hero in Greek mythology, Hercules. Over the next several days your child will hear more about the twelve labors of Hercules, specifically his fight with the Nemean lion and his search for the golden apples of the Hesperides. Your child will also hear about the riddle of the Sphinx and the story of Atalanta, a swift-footed huntress who refused to marry.

Below are some suggestions for activities that you may do at home to reinforce what your child is learning about Greek myths over the next several days.

1. Hercules

Have your child share with you what s/he has learned about Hercules. Share with your child that the name "Hercules" is actually the better-known Roman pronunciation of this mythical hero. In Greek "Hercules" is pronounced "Heracles" [HER-uh-kleez]. You may wish to search at the library or online for text or more details about Hercules' other labors to share with your child.

2. Sayings and Phrases: Back to the Drawing Board

Your child will learn the saying "back to the drawing board" in relation to the myth of Hercules and the golden apples. Hercules does not know where these apples are, but has heard stories that they can be found to the west. He travels to the west but does not find the apples. As a result he has to start his search all over again or has to go "back to the drawing board." Talk with your child about other situations where one might say "back to the drawing board" when something doesn't work out at first.

3. The Riddle of the Sphinx

Talk with your child about the riddle of the Sphinx, a winged, mythical creature with the body of a lion and the face of a woman. Have your child tell you the riddle and share the answer with you after you have guessed. If you know of any other riddles, share them with your child, or brainstorm with your child to create new riddles about the Greek myths s/he has heard.

4. Atalanta

Ask your child to tell you about Atalanta, the swift-footed huntress. Discuss with your child how the goddess Aphrodite helped one of Atalanta's suitors trick her, sharing that the Greek gods and goddesses were believed to have often interfered in the lives of mortals. Share with your child other myths you may know of where the Greek gods or goddesses interfered in the lives of others.

5. Words to Use

Below is a list of some of the words that your child will be learning about and using. Try to use these words as they come up in everyday speech with your child.

- *labors*—Hercules had to complete twelve difficult labors or tasks.

- *reputation*—Hercules cleared his reputation, or the people's opinion of him, as ill-tempered after he completed those twelve labors.

- *posed*—The Sphinx posed her difficult riddle to any traveler who walked the road to Thebes.

- *resist*—Atalanta was unable to resist the golden apples.

6. Read Aloud Each Day

It is very important that you read to your child each day. Please refer to the list of books and other resources sent home with the previous family letter, recommending resources related to Greek myths and the ancient Greek civilization.

Be sure to let your child know how much you enjoy hearing about what s/he has learned at school.

Directions: Write the beginning, middle, and end of your myth on the following lines. Be sure to write complete sentences that begin with a capital letter and end with the correct punctuation.

_____

_____

_____

_____

_____

_____

_____

_____

_____

_____

_____

_____

_____

_____

_____

_____

Directions: Use this worksheet to write your myth. Fill in the blanks with the information you have chosen to include in your myth. On the back of this paper, draw a picture of a scene from your myth.

_____

Myth Title

Written and Illustrated by _____

Long ago there was _____

_____ who lived

_____

_____ .

One day, _____

_____

_____ .

Then the god/goddess (name) _____

_____

_____

_____ .

After that _____

_____

_____

_____ .

And that is why/how _____

_____

_____ .

Name _____

Title: _____

Directions: Use this worksheet for your writing and drawing. Remember to write complete sentences that begin with a capital letter and end with the correct punctuation.

Name _____

. ? !

The cat ran.

Name _____

Title: _____

Directions: Use this worksheet for your writing and drawing. Remember to write complete sentences that begin with a capital letter and end with the correct punctuation.

_____

_____

_____

_____

_____

_____

_____

_____

_____

_____

_____

Name _____

Directions: These six pictures show events from the myth of Hercules. Cut out the six pictures. Think about what is happening in each one. Put the pictures in order to show the sequence of events of the myth. Glue them in the correct order on a piece of paper.

Directions: Listen to your teacher's instructions.

1.

2.

3.

4.

5.

6.

7.

8.

9.

10.

11.

12.

13.

14.

15.

Name _____

Directions: Listen to each sentence read by the teacher. If the sentence is true, circle the smiling face. If the sentence is false, circle the frowning face.

1.

2.

3.

4.

5.

6.

7.

8.

9.

10.

Name _____

Directions: Listen as your teacher reads each sentence. Think about the answer. Write words, phrases, or sentences that come to mind when you hear the question.

1. Who was the most outrageous character you heard about in the Greek myths? Make sure to explain why.

    _____

    _____

    _____

    _____

    _____

2. How did the ancient Greeks explain the name of the Aegean Sea?

    _____

    _____

    _____

    _____

    _____

3. Describe one nonhuman creature you heard about in these Greek myths.

_____

_____

_____

_____

_____

4. Tell about the supernatural powers of one of the characters you heard about in the Greek myths.

_____

_____

_____

_____

_____

CORE KNOWLEDGE LANGUAGE ARTS

SERIES EDITOR-IN-CHIEF
E. D. Hirsch, Jr.

PRESIDENT
Linda Bevilacqua

EDITORIAL STAFF
Carolyn Gosse, Senior Editor - Preschool
Khara Turnbull, Materials Development Manager
Michelle L. Warner, Senior Editor - Listening & Learning

Mick Anderson
Robin Blackshire
Maggie Buchanan
Paula Coyner
Sue Fulton
Sara Hunt
Erin Kist
Robin Luecke
Rosie McCormick
Cynthia Peng
Liz Pettit
Ellen Sadler
Deborah Samley
Diane Auger Smith
Sarah Zelinke

DESIGN AND GRAPHICS STAFF
Scott Ritchie, Creative Director

Kim Berrall
Michael Donegan
Liza Greene
Matt Leech
Bridget Moriarty
Lauren Pack

CONSULTING PROJECT MANAGEMENT SERVICES
ScribeConcepts.com

ADDITIONAL CONSULTING SERVICES
Ang Blanchette
Dorrit Green
Carolyn Pinkerton

ACKNOWLEDGMENTS
These materials are the result of the work, advice, and encouragement of numerous individuals over many years. Some of those singled out here already know the depth of our gratitude; others may be surprised to find themselves thanked publicly for help they gave quietly and generously for the sake of the enterprise alone. To helpers named and unnamed we are deeply grateful.

CONTRIBUTORS TO EARLIER VERSIONS OF THESE MATERIALS
Susan B. Albaugh, Kazuko Ashizawa, Nancy Braier, Kathryn M. Cummings, Michelle De Groot, Diana Espinal, Mary E. Forbes, Michael L. Ford, Ted Hirsch, Danielle Knecht, James K. Lee, Diane Henry Leipzig, Martha G. Mack, Liana Mahoney, Isabel McLean, Steve Morrison, Juliane K. Munson, Elizabeth B. Rasmussen, Laura Tortorelli, Rachael L. Shaw, Sivan B. Sherman, Miriam E. Vidaver, Catherine S. Whittington, Jeannette A. Williams

We would like to extend special recognition to Program Directors Matthew Davis and Souzanne Wright who were instrumental to the early development of this program.

SCHOOLS
We are truly grateful to the teachers, students, and administrators of the following schools for their willingness to field test these materials and for their invaluable advice: Capitol View Elementary, Challenge Foundation Academy (IN), Community Academy Public Charter School, Lake Lure Classical Academy, Lepanto Elementary School, New Holland Core Knowledge Academy, Paramount School of Excellence, Pioneer Challenge Foundation Academy, New York City PS 26R (The Carteret School), PS 30X (Wilton School), PS 50X (Clara Barton School), PS 96Q, PS 102X (Joseph O. Loretan), PS 104Q (The Bays Water), PS 214K (Michael Friedsam), PS 223Q (Lyndon B. Johnson School), PS 308K (Clara Cardwell), PS 333Q (Goldie Maple Academy), Sequoyah Elementary School, South Shore Charter Public School, Spartanburg Charter School, Steed Elementary School, Thomas Jefferson Classical Academy, Three Oaks Elementary, West Manor Elementary.

And a special thanks to the CKLA Pilot Coordinators Anita Henderson, Yasmin Lugo-Hernandez, and Susan Smith, whose suggestions and day-to-day support to teachers using these materials in their classrooms was critical.

Domain 5: The War of 1812

Tell It Again!™ Workbook

Listening & Learning™ Strand
GRADE 2

Amplify learning.

Core Knowledge®

Name _____

Directions: Use this paper for your writing and drawing. Remember to write complete sentences that begin with a capital letter and end with the correct punctuation.

_____

_____

_____

_____

Dear Family Member,

During the next several days, your child will be hearing stories about the War of 1812. S/he will learn about the events that led to the war, how Great Britain was already involved in the Napoleonic Wars with France, how British soldiers captured Americans and made them fight for the British navy, and about the famous American battleship, the USS *Constitution.* S/he will also learn about some geographic locations, as well as some important people involved in the War of 1812, including President James Madison and his wife Dolley Madison. Below are some suggestions for activities that you may do at home to reinforce what your child is learning about the War of 1812.

1. James Madison

Talk with your child about this important historical figure. James Madison was the fourth president of the United States. Point out that he is one of the Founding Fathers who wrote the Constitution. Discuss the contributions that he made. Ask your child what role James Madison had in the War of 1812.

2. Dolley Madison

Your child will learn that Dolley Madison was married to James Madison. She was previously married to a man named John Payne; however, her first husband and one of her young sons died of yellow fever. Dolley Madison was known as an excellent hostess. She was the first First Lady.

3. USS *Constitution*/"Old Ironsides"

Your child will learn about the famous United States battleship, the USS *Constitution.* The USS *Constitution* is the oldest American battleship that is still afloat, and is now located in the Boston harbor. S/he will also learn about the *Constitution*'s nickname, "Old Ironsides," and how it got that name. Take this opportunity to talk to your child about the important job of the military, and the navy in particular, especially if you have family members who are veterans or who actively serve.

4. Words to Use

Below is a list of some of the words that your child will be learning about and using. Try to use these words as they come up in everyday speech with your child.

- *impressment*—The practice of British soldiers forcing other countries' soldiers into the British navy

- *navy*—The part of the military that protects the nation's interests at sea
- *role*—Jean Lafitte is a pirate who played an important part, or role, in the Battle of New Orleans.
- *economy*—The economy of the United States was largely dependent on trade with Great Britain and France.

6. Read Aloud Each Day

It is very important that you read with your child every day. Set aside time to read to your child and also time to listen to your child read to you. I have attached a list of recommended trade books related to the War of 1812 that may be found at the library.

Be sure to let your child know how much you enjoy hearing about what s/he has learned in school.

Recommended Resources for The War of 1812

Trade Book List

1. *The American Flag (True Books: American History),* by Elaine Landau (Children's Press, 2008) ISBN 978-0531147757

2. *A More Perfect Union: The Story of Our Constitution,* by Betsy Maestro (HarperCollins, 1990) ISBN 978-0688101923

3. *An Army of Two,* by Janet Greeson and illustrated by Patricia Rose Mulvihill (First Avenue Editions, 1991) ISBN 978-0876145470

4. *The Battle of New Orleans: The Drummer's Story,* by Freddi Evans (Pelican Publishing, 2005) ISBN 978-1589803008

5. *The Biggest (and Best) Flag That Ever Flew,* by Rebecca C. Jones (Tidewater Publishers, 1988) ISBN 978-0870334405

6. *The Bill of Rights,* by Christine Taylor-Butler (Children's Press, 2008) ISBN 978-0531147771

7. *The Boy Who Saved the Town,* by Brenda Seabrooke (Schiffer Publishing, 1990) ISBN 978-0870334054

8. *The Constitution of the United States (True Books),* by Christine Taylor-Butler (Children's Press, 2008) ISBN 978-0531147795

9. *Dolley Madison (First Biographies),* by Jan Mader (Capstone Press, 2007) ISBN 978-0736867016

10. *Dolley Madison: First Lady of the United States (Focus on Women in U.S. History: Primary Source Readers),* by Melissa Carosella (Teacher Created Materials, 2011) ISBN 978-1433315046

11. *Dolley Madison: Her Life, Letters, and Legacy,* by Holly Shulman and David Mattern (Rosen Publishing Group; 2002) ISBN 978-0823957491

12. *Dolley Madison Saves George Washington,* by Don Brown (Houghton Mifflin Books for Children, 2007) ISBN 978-0618411993

13. *The Flag Maker,* by Susan Campbell Bartoletti (Houghton Mifflin Books for Children, 2004) ISBN 978-0618267576

14. *Francis Scott Key and "The Star-Spangled Banner,"* by Lynnea Bowdish and illustrated by Harry Burman (Mondo, 2002) ISBN 978-1590341957

15. *Francis Scott Key's "Star-Spangled Banner," (Step into Reading),* by Monica Kulling and illustrated by Richard Walz (Random House Books for Young Readers, 2012) ISBN 978-0375867255

16. *If You Were There When They Signed the Constitution,* by Elizabeth Levy and illustrated by Joan Holub (Scholastic, 1992) ISBN 978-0590451598

17. *James Madison,* by Jill K. Mulhall (Teacher Created Materials, 2008) ISBN 978-0743989084

18. *James Madison: Founding Father,* by Lynn George (Rosen Publishing Group, 2002) ISBN 978-0823963829

19. *Jean Laffite: The Pirate Who Saved America,* by Susan Goldman Rubin and illustrated by Jeff Himmelman (Abram Books for Young Readers, 2012) ISBN 978-0810997332

20. *Meet Caroline,* by Kathleen Ernst (American Girl, 2012) ISBN 978-1593698829

21. *Millie Cooper's Ride: A True Story from History,* by Marc Simmons (University of New Mexico Press, 2002) ISBN 978-0826329257

22. *The National Anthem (True Books: American History),* by Elaine Landau (Children's Press, 2008) ISBN 978-0531147832

23. *A Picture Book of Dolley and James Madison,* by David A. Adler and Michael S. Adler and illustrated by Ronald Himler (Holiday House, 2009) ISBN 978-0823420094

24. *Pirates Past Noon (Magic Tree House, No. 4),* by Mary Pope Osborne (Random House, 1994) ISBN 978-0679824251

25. *The Star-Spangled Banner,* by Peter Spier (Dragonfly Books, 1992) ISBN 978-0440406976

26. *Shh! We're Writing the Constitution,* by Jean Fritz (Puffin, 1997) ISBN 978-0698116245

27. *Sisters of Scituate Light,* by Stephen Krensky (Dutton Children's Books, 2008) ISBN 978-0525477921

28. *The Star-Spangled Banner in Translation: What It Really Means (Fact Finders: Kids' Translations),* by Elizabeth Raum (Capstone Press, 2008) ISBN 978-1429628471

29. *The War of 1812: Expanding & Preserving the Union (Primary Source Readers),* by Jill K. Mulhall (Teacher Created Materials, 2008) ISBN 978-0743989077

30. *The War of 1812: The New American Nation Goes to War with England,* by Mark Beyer (Rosen Publishing, 2004) ISBN 978-0823942619

31. *The War of 1812 (Primary Sources of American Wars),* by Georgene Poulakidas (PowerKids, 2006) ISBN 978-1404226814

32. *Washington Is Burning! The War of 1812,* by Alvin R. Cunningham (Perfection Learning, 2003) ISBN 978-0822560500

33. *Washington Is Burning (On My Own History),* by Marty Rhodes Figley and illustrated by Craig Orback (Lerner Books, 2006) ISBN 978-0822560500

34. *We the Kids: The Preamble to the Constitution of the United States,* by David Catrow (Puffin, 2005) ISBN 978-014202764

Websites

Family Resources

1. Chalmette Battlefield National Park
   http://www.nps.gov/jela/chalmette-battlefield.htm

2. Fort McHenry National Park
   http://www.nps.gov/fomc/index.htm

3. The Flag House and Star-Spangled Banner Museum
   http://www.flaghouse.org

4. The Star-Spangled Banner Exhibit at the Smithsonian
   http://americanhistory.si.edu/starspangledbanner

5. Video Clips on the Star Spangled Banner
   http://www.youtube.com/watch?v=zDKfw8nysLA
   http://www.youtube.com/watch?v=iwsq7frSB5Q

6. Montpelier Historic Website
   http://www.montpelier.org

7. PBS Film on Dolley Madison
   http://www.pbs.org/wgbh/americanexperience/films/dolley

8. Official Bicentennial Website
   http://www.visit1812.com

9. The U.S. Capitol Visitor's Center
   http://www.visitthecapitol.gov/Exhibitions/online

10. USS Constitution Museum
    http://www.ussconstitutionmuseum.org

11. The James Madison Museum
    http://www.thejamesmadisonmuseum.org

12. The Papers of James Madison
    www.virginia.edu/pjm

13. The White House
    http://www.whitehouse.gov/about/presidents/jamesmadison

14. The Crafty Classroom
    http://www.thecraftyclassroom.com/
    HomeschoolPrintablesNotebookingPatriotic.html

15. Hold the Fort (Online Game)
    http://www.nps.gov/fomc/holdthefort

Student Resources

16. Interactive Map: America in 1812
    http://bit.ly/XYmKBy

17. Music and Lyrics to "The Battle of New Orleans"
    http://kids.niehs.nih.gov/lyrics/battleof.htm

18. Music and Lyrics to the Star Spangled Banner
    http://kids.niehs.nih.gov/lyrics/spangle.htm

19. The White House Interactive Tour
    http://www.whitehouse.gov/about/interactive-tour

20. A Sailor's Life for Me! (Online Game)
    http://asailorslifeforme.org

Name _____

War Hawks	Merchants

Name _____

Open/ Introduction	
Opinion/ Position	
Because	
Also	
Close/ Conclusion	

Name _____

Directions: Use this paper for your writing and drawing. Remember to write complete sentences that begin with a capital letter and end with the correct punctuation.

_____

_____

_____

_____

Name _____

Directions: Follow your teacher's instructions to show what you learned. List important details about James Madison and Dolley Madison by drawing or writing in each column.

James Madison	Dolley Madison

Name _____

Directions: Use this paper for your writing and drawing. Remember to write complete sentences that begin with a capital letter and end with the correct punctuation.

_____

_____

_____

_____

Name _____

1. —————, James Madison asked some soldiers to stay with Mrs. Madison and to keep her safe.

2. —————, The British sent an army of about four-thousand men to the capital.

3. —————, James Madison rode off to be with his army.

4. —————, James Madison told Mrs. Madison to stay in the President's House.

1. —————, the British Soldiers set fire to the President's House.

2. —————, Dolley Madison escaped just in the nick of time.

3. —————, some of the British soldiers sat down at the dinner table and enjoyed a tasty meal.

4. —————, Dolley Madison asked the workers in the house to help her remove a painting of George Washington.

The War of 1812

Name _____

Directions: Use this paper for your writing and drawing. Remember to write complete sentences that begin with a capital letter and end with the correct punctuation.

_____

_____

_____

_____

The War of 1812

Dear Family Member,

I hope your child has enjoyed learning about the War of 1812. Over the next several days, s/he will learn about the British's three-part plan to defeat the United States, including attacks on Lake Erie and in Washington, D.C., the Battle at Fort McHenry, and the Battle of New Orleans. They will also learn that the Battle of New Orleans was actually fought after the war had ended. S/he will also learn about some geographic locations, as well as some important people involved in the War of 1812, such as Francis Scott Key, Mary Pickersgill, and Andrew Jackson.

Below are some suggestions for activities that you may do at home to reinforce what your child is learning about the War of 1812.

1. The President's House

Today your child heard about the British attack on Washington, D.C., during which the British set fire to many official buildings in the capital, including the President's House. They learned how Dolley Madison escaped before the soldiers arrived and how she saved a portrait of George Washington. You might explain that the President's House is now known as the White House.

2. Francis Scott Key

Your child will also learn about the Battle at Fort McHenry, and how Francis Scott Key watched the "rockets' red glare" and "bombs bursting in air" from the harbor. S/he will also hear how Francis Scott Key was inspired to write a poem about it. The poem he wrote became our national anthem, "The Star-Spangled Banner." Ask your child about the giant flag that Mary Pickersgill made to fly over Fort McHenry that day.

3. Song: "The Star-Spangled Banner"

Listen to the song "The Star-Spangled Banner" with your child. Discuss with your child that this song is our national anthem. It was written by Francis Scott Key during the War of 1812. Talk about times when you might sing the national anthem. Ask them to tell you what they learned about what you should do anytime you hear the song played in a public place. The next time you hear the song played at a ball game or other event, ask your child who wrote "The Star-Spangled Banner."

4. Song: "Battle of New Orleans"

Listen to the song "The Battle of New Orleans" with your child. Discuss what the song is about and how it tells the story of the War of 1812.

5. Andrew Jackson

Have your child talk about the Andrew Jackson's role in the Battle of New Orleans. Discuss how General Andrew Jackson put together an army of militiamen, soldiers, Native Americans, African Americans, farmers, and even pirates to win the Battle of New Orleans. You might want to explain that Andrew Jackson later became the seventh president of the United States.

6. Using a Map

Help your child locate the areas they learned about on a map of the United States, including the Mississippi River, New Orleans, Canada, Baltimore, and Washington, D.C. Have your child tell you about Britain's three-part plan to defeat the United States.

7. Sayings and Phrases: Where There's a Will There's a Way

Your child will learn the saying "where there's a will there's a way" in relation to how Andrew Jackson did whatever it took to win the Battle of New Orleans. Talk with your child about its meaning. Share something that you have accomplished because of your determination. Find opportunities to use this saying again and again.

8. Words to Use

Below is a list of some of the words that your child has been learning about and using. Try to use these words as they come up in everyday speech with your child.

- *navigator*—The ship's navigator helped the captain locate the harbor.
- *truce*—One British officer gave his sword to a U.S. officer as a sign of truce.
- *treaty*—Andrew Jackson received the news that a peace treaty had been signed.
- *surrender*—The soldiers had to surrender when they knew they couldn't win.

9. Read Aloud Each Day

It is very important that you read with your child every day. Set aside time to read to your child and also time to listen to your child read to you. I have attached a list of recommended trade books related to the War of 1812 that may be found at the library.

Be sure to let your child know how much you enjoy hearing about what s/he has learned in school.

Name _____

The Star-Spangled Banner

During the War of 1812, Francis Scott Key (1779–1843) witnessed the all-night bombardment of Ft. McHenry in Maryland. Despite the fierce assault, Key was elated to see in the morning that the American flag was still proudly waving over the fort, meaning that the fort was still manned. Inspired, he wrote this poem to celebrate the event. "The Star-Spangled Banner" was declared the national anthem in 1931.

Melody by John Stafford Smith
Lyrics by Francis Scott Key

Name _____

Directions: Use this paper for your writing and drawing. Remember to write complete sentences that begin with a capital letter and end with the correct punctuation.

_____

_____

_____

_____

Directions: Use this paper for your writing and drawing. Remember to write complete sentences that begin with a capital letter and end with the correct punctuation.

_____

_____

_____

_____

Name _____

Directions: Use this paper for your writing and drawing. Remember to write complete sentences that begin with a capital letter and end with the correct punctuation.

_____

_____

_____

_____

_____

Name _____

Directions: Write your topic sentence in the first rectangle. In the second, third, and fourth rectangles write something about them, where, and when. Write why they are important in the fifth rectangle.

Who?	
What?	
Where?	
When?	
Why?	

Name _____

1.

2.

3.

4.

5.

6.

7.

8.

9.

10.

Directions: Listen to your teacher's instructions.

11. ☺ ☹

12. ☺ ☹

13. ☺ ☹

14. ☺ ☹

15. ☺ ☹

Name _____

Directions: These pictures show some important people and events from the War of 1812. Place the number of the question in a box by the appropriate person or event.

Dolley Madison

James Madison

Andrew Jackson

Francis Scott Key

U.S.S. *Constitution*

President's House

Name _____

Directions: Listen to your teacher's instructions.

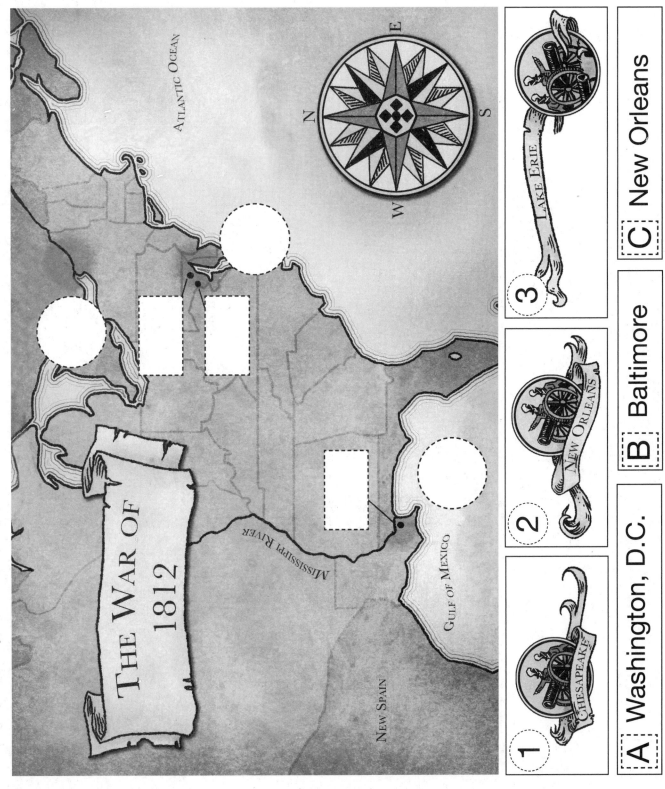

ATLANTIC OCEAN

N
E
S
W

THE WAR OF 1812

MISSISSIPPI RIVER

NEW SPAIN

GULF OF MEXICO

3 LAKE ERIE

2 NEW ORLEANS

1 CHESAPEAKE

A Washington, D.C.

B Baltimore

C New Orleans

Name _____

Directions: Read each sentence. Think about the answer to the question or statement. Write a complete sentence to answer each question or statement.

1. Why was the War of 1812 called the second war for independence?

    _____

    _____

    _____

2. How is "The Star-Spangled Banner" connected to the War of 1812?

    _____

    _____

    _____

3. What was impressment?

    _____

    _____

    _____

4. Why did the British want to control New Orleans?

_____

_____

_____

5. What was the most interesting thing you learned about the War of 1812?

_____

_____

_____

CORE KNOWLEDGE LANGUAGE ARTS

SERIES EDITOR-IN-CHIEF
E. D. Hirsch, Jr.

PRESIDENT
Linda Bevilacqua

EDITORIAL STAFF
Carolyn Gosse, Senior Editor - Preschool
Khara Turnbull, Materials Development Manager
Michelle L. Warner, Senior Editor - Listening & Learning

Mick Anderson
Robin Blackshire
Maggie Buchanan
Paula Coyner
Sue Fulton
Sara Hunt
Erin Kist
Robin Luecke
Rosie McCormick
Cynthia Peng
Liz Pettit
Ellen Sadler
Deborah Samley
Diane Auger Smith
Sarah Zelinke

DESIGN AND GRAPHICS STAFF
Scott Ritchie, Creative Director

Kim Berrall
Michael Donegan
Liza Greene
Matt Leech
Bridget Moriarty
Lauren Pack

CONSULTING PROJECT MANAGEMENT SERVICES
ScribeConcepts.com

ADDITIONAL CONSULTING SERVICES
Ang Blanchette
Dorrit Green
Carolyn Pinkerton

ACKNOWLEDGMENTS

These materials are the result of the work, advice, and encouragement of numerous individuals over many years. Some of those singled out here already know the depth of our gratitude; others may be surprised to find themselves thanked publicly for help they gave quietly and generously for the sake of the enterprise alone. To helpers named and unnamed we are deeply grateful.

CONTRIBUTORS TO EARLIER VERSIONS OF THESE MATERIALS
Susan B. Albaugh, Kazuko Ashizawa, Nancy Braier, Kathryn M. Cummings, Michelle De Groot, Diana Espinal, Mary E. Forbes, Michael L. Ford, Ted Hirsch, Danielle Knecht, James K. Lee, Diane Henry Leipzig, Martha G. Mack, Liana Mahoney, Isabel McLean, Steve Morrison, Juliane K. Munson, Elizabeth B. Rasmussen, Laura Tortorelli, Rachael L. Shaw, Sivan B. Sherman, Miriam E. Vidaver, Catherine S. Whittington, Jeannette A. Williams

We would like to extend special recognition to Program Directors Matthew Davis and Souzanne Wright who were instrumental to the early development of this program.

SCHOOLS
We are truly grateful to the teachers, students, and administrators of the following schools for their willingness to field test these materials and for their invaluable advice: Capitol View Elementary, Challenge Foundation Academy (IN), Community Academy Public Charter School, Lake Lure Classical Academy, Lepanto Elementary School, New Holland Core Knowledge Academy, Paramount School of Excellence, Pioneer Challenge Foundation Academy, New York City PS 26R (The Carteret School), PS 30X (Wilton School), PS 50X (Clara Barton School), PS 96Q, PS 102X (Joseph O. Loretan), PS 104Q (The Bays Water), PS 214K (Michael Friedsam), PS 223Q (Lyndon B. Johnson School), PS 308K (Clara Cardwell), PS 333Q (Goldie Maple Academy), Sequoyah Elementary School, South Shore Charter Public School, Spartanburg Charter School, Steed Elementary School, Thomas Jefferson Classical Academy, Three Oaks Elementary, West Manor Elementary.

And a special thanks to the CKLA Pilot Coordinators Anita Henderson, Yasmin Lugo-Hernandez, and Susan Smith, whose suggestions and day-to-day support to teachers using these materials in their classrooms was critical.

CREDITS

Every effort has been taken to trace and acknowledge copyrights. The editors tender their apologies for any accidental infringement where copyright has proved untraceable. They would be pleased to insert the appropriate acknowledgment in any subsequent edition of this publication. Trademarks and trade names are shown in this publication for illustrative purposes only and are the property of their respective owners. The references to trademarks and trade names given herein do not affect their validity.

The Word Work exercises are based on the work of Beck, McKeown, and Kucan in Bringing Words to Life *(The Guilford Press, 2002).*

All photographs are used under license from Shutterstock, Inc. unless otherwise noted.

EXPERT REVIEWER
J. Chris Arndt

WRITERS
Rosie McCormick

ILLUSTRATORS AND IMAGE SOURCES
Take-Home Icon: Core Knowledge Staff; 1B-1: Shutterstock; 2B-3: Shutterstock; 4B-1: Shutterstock; 5B-2: Shutterstock; 6B-2: Shutterstock; 7B-1: Shutterstock; 8B-1: Shutterstock; DA-2 (Dolly Madison): public domain; DA-2 (James Madison): public domain; DA-2 (Andrew Jackson): Library of Congress, Prints & Photographs Division, LC-USZC4-6466; DA-2 (Francis Scot Key): Library of Congress, Prints & Photographs Division, NYWT&S Collection, LC-DIG-ds-00032a; DA-2 (USS Constitution): USS Constitution vs Guerriere by Michel Felice Corne (1752-1845). Image courtesy of the Beverley R. Robinson Collection, U.S. Naval Academy Museum; FDA-2 (White House): Library of Congress, Prints and Photographs, LC-DIG-ppmsca-09502; DA-2 (Dolly Madison) (Answer Key): public domain; DA-2 (James Madison) (Answer Key): public domain; DA-2 (Andrew Jackson) (Answer Key): Library of Congress, Prints & Photographs Division, LC-USZC4-6466; DA-2 (Francis Scot Key) (Answer Key): Library of Congress, Prints & Photographs Division, NYWT&S Collection, LC-DIG-ds-00032a; DA-2 (USS Constitution) (Answer Key): USS Constitution vs Guerriere by Michel Felice Corne (1752-1845). Image courtesy of the Beverley R. Robinson Collection, U.S. Naval Academy Museum; DA-2 (White House) (Answer Key): Library of Congress, Prints and Photographs, LC-DIG-ppmsca-09502; DA-3: Erika Baird; DA-3 (Answer Key): Erika Baird

Regarding the Shutterstock items listed above, please note: "No person or entity shall falsely represent, expressly or by way of reasonable implication, that the content herein was created by that person or entity, or any person other than the copyright holder(s) of that content."

Domain 6: Cycles in Nature

Tell It Again!™ Workbook

Listening & Learning™ Strand

GRADE 2

Amplify learning.

Core Knowledge®

Dear Family Member,

During the next several days, your child will learn about cycles and explore some of the different types of cycles that occur in nature. Your child will be introduced to the reasons why we have four seasons on planet Earth, and to the different seasonal changes that affect the life cycles of plants and trees. Below are some suggestions for activities that you may do at home to reinforce what your child is learning about cycles in nature.

1. Personal Connections

Share with your child your favorite season and the different experiences from your own childhood connected with seasonal changes. Emphasize the changes observed in plants and animals. Ask your child what favorite memories s/he has of a particular season shared with you and your family.

2. Draw and Write

Have your child draw and/or write what s/he has learned about seasonal cycles and the life cycles of plants. Ask questions to help your child use the vocabulary learned at school.

3. Words to Use

Below is a list of some of the words that your child will be learning about and using. Try to use these words as they come up in everyday speech with your child.

- *revolve*—It takes one year for Earth to revolve around the sun.

- *hibernation*—Some animals have longer periods of winter hibernation than others.

- *cycles*—Planet Earth has many cycles, such as day and night, the seasons, and life cycles of plants.

4. Read Aloud Each Day

Set aside time to read aloud to your child every day. The local library has many books on cycles in nature. A list of books and other resources relevant to this topic is attached to this letter.

Be sure to let your child know how much you enjoy hearing about what s/he has been learning at school.

Recommended Resources for Cycles in Nature

Trade Book List

Seasonal Cycles

1. *Earth Cycles,* by Michael Elsohn Ross (Millbrook Press, 2001) ISBN 978-0761319771

2. *Four Seasons Make a Year,* by Anne Rockwell (Walker & Company, 2004) ISBN 978-0802788832

3. *How Do Birds Find Their Way?,* by Roma Gans (Harper Collins, 1996) ISBN 978-0064451505

4. *The Reasons for Seasons,* by Gail Gibbons (Holiday House, 1995) ISBN 978-0823412389

5. *Red Leaf, Yellow Leaf,* by Lois Ehlert (Harcourt, Inc., 1991) ISBN 978-0152661977

6. *What Makes Day and Night,* by Franklyn Branley (Harper Collins, 1986) ISBN 978-0064450508

Plant and Animal Life Cycles

7. *Butterfly (How Does it Grow?),* by Jinny Johnson (Smart Apple Media, 2010) ISBN 978-1599203522

8. *Frogs (How Does it Grow?),* by Jinny Johnson (Smart Apple Media, 2010) ISBN 978-1599203553

9. *From Caterpillar to Butterfly (Let's-Read-and-Find-Out-Science),* by Deborah Heiligman (Harper Collins Publishers, 1996) ISBN 978-0064451291

10. *From Seed to Plant,* by Gail Gibbons (Holiday House, 1991) ISBN 978-0823410255

11. *From Seed to Sunflower,* by Dr. Gerald Legg (Franklin Watts, 1998) ISBN 978-0531153345

12. *How a Seed Grows,* by Helene J. Jordan (Harper Collins, 2000) ISBN 978-0064451079

13. *The Life Cycle of an Oak Tree,* by Linda Tagliaferro (Capstone Press, 2007) ISBN 978-0736867115

14. *A Log's Life,* by Wendy Pfeffer (Aladdin Paperbacks, 1997) ISBN 978-1416934837

15. *Monarch Butterfly,* by Gail Gibbons (Holiday House, 1995) ISBN 978-0823409099

16. *A Nest Full of Eggs,* by Priscilla Belz Jenkins (Harper Collins, 1995) ISBN 978-0064451277

17. *One Bean,* by Anne Rockwell (Walker Publishing Company, 1998) ISBN 978-0802775726

18. *The Reason for a Flower,* by Ruth Heller (Penguin Putnam Books for Young Readers, 1999) ISBN 978-0698115590

Water Cycle

19. *Down Comes the Rain (Let's-Read-and-Find-Out-Science),* by Franklyn M. Branley (Harper Collins Publishers, 1997) ISBN 978-0064451666

20. *The Snowflake: A Water Cycle Story,* by Neil Waldman (Milbrook Press, 2003) ISBN 978-0761323471

21. *Water (Nature's Cycles)* [Spanish & English], by Dana Meachen Rau (Marshall Cavendish Corporation, 2010) ISBN 978-0761447924

22. *The Water Cycle,* by Helen Frost (Pebble Books, 2000) ISBN 978-0736804097

23. *The Water Cycle,* by Rebecca Olien (Capstone Press, 2005) ISBN 978-0736851824

24. *Water, Water Everywhere,* Mark J. Rauzon and Cynthia Overbeck Bix (Sierra Club Books for Children, 1994) ISBN 978-0871563835

Websites and Other Resources

Student Resources

1. Interactive Earth Rotation
   http://www.bbc.co.uk/schools/scienceclips/ages/9_10/earth_sun_moon.shtml

2. Creature Feature: American Bullfrog
   http://kids.nationalgeographic.com/kids/animals/creaturefeature/american-bullfrog

3. Creature Feature: Penguin
   http://kids.nationalgeographic.com/kids/animals/creaturefeature/adelie-penguin

4. Caterpillar to a Butterfly
   http://www.youtube.com/watch?v=5Tvl6wz7e9M

5. Water Cycle Song
   http://www.youtube.com/watch?v=KQ8KRznrXiA

6. How Water Changes
   http://www.youtube.com/watch?v=oaCUyZw4Tjo

Family Resources

1. The Water Cycle
   http://www.sciencekids.co.nz/sciencefacts/weather/thewatercycle.htm

2. *March of the Penguins* DVD, with Morgan Freeman (Warner Bros., 2005) ASIN: B000NJUYHM

Name _____

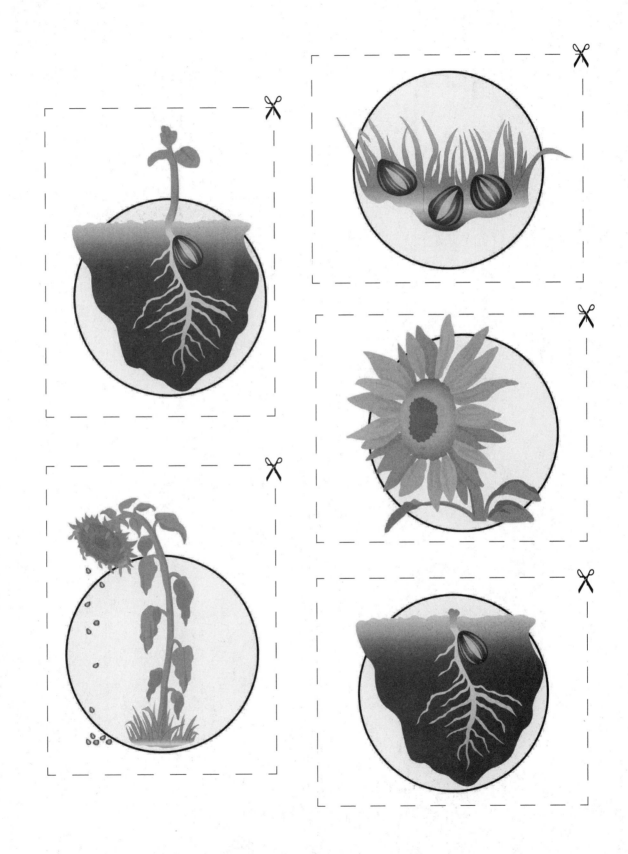

Directions: Cut out the pictures of the plant at various stages. Sequence the pictures, starting with the beginning of the plant life cycle. Then, glue or tape the pictures in the correct order onto a separate sheet of paper.

Name _____

Directions: Write some characteristics that only the flowering plant life cycle has in the circle with its name. Write some characteristics that only the tree life cycle has in the circle with its name. In the overlapping middle section, write the characteristics that both of these plant life cycles have in common.

Tree Life Cycle

Flowering Plant Life Cycle

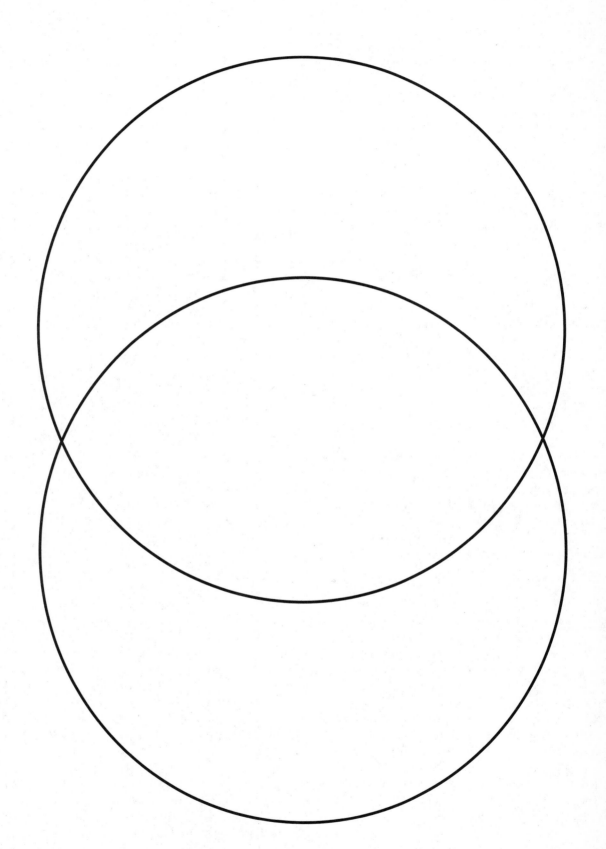

Dear Family Member,

I hope your child has enjoyed learning about cycles in nature, specifically the seasonal cycle and the life cycles of flowering plants and trees. Over the next several days, s/he will learn about the life cycle of a chicken, frog, and butterfly. In addition, s/he will be introduced to another cycle: the water cycle. Below are some suggestions for activities that you may do at home to reinforce what your child is learning about cycles in nature.

1. Animal Life Cycle Picture Hunt

If you have old magazines around your house, have your child page through them and find pictures of animals to cut out. Your child will learn the stages of the life cycle of the chicken (egg, chick, adult), frog (egg, tadpole/larva, adult), and butterfly (egg, caterpillar/larva, chrysalis/pupa, adult). See if your child can identify which stage of the life cycle s/he observes in each picture.

2. Draw and Write

Have your child draw and/or write about the stages of the water cycle: evaporation, condensation, and precipitation. S/he may also wish to share the water cycle song learned at school. Ask questions to help your child use the vocabulary learned at school.

3. What Season Am I?

Have your child use adjectives in full sentence questions to pose questions such as:

I am the time of year when cold, white snow falls from the sky, and the chilling wind blows. What season am I?

4. Personal Connections

Ask your child about the types of precipitation: rain, snow, sleet, and hail. Share with your child your favorite type of precipitation and/or a special childhood memory related to it. Ask your child about a favorite memory s/he has related to a particular type of precipitation. Ask your child why precipitation is important.

5. Cloud Gazing

Set aside a period of time during the day to view different cloud formations with your child. Ask your child to name the different cloud formations and to explain how s/he is able to determine these by their shape: cirrus (wispy, feathery clouds high in the sky), cumulus (round, puffy clouds), and stratus (layered grey clouds that can cover the whole sky and usually bring rain). Talk about the kind of weather that different types of clouds indicate.

6. Words to Use

Below is a list of some of the words that your child will be learning about and using. Try to use these words as they come up in everyday speech with your child.

- *metamorphosis*—The drastic set of changes that a tadpole completes to become an adult frog is an example of metamorphosis.

- *water cycle*—Earth's water cycle involves three stages: evaporation, condensation, and precipitation.

- *evaporation*—We had to refill our swimming pool because of the evaporation of some of the water.

- *humidity*—There is high humidity in the tropical rainforests.

7. Read Aloud Each Day

Set aside time to read with your child every day. Please refer to the list of books and other resources sent home with the previous family letter, recommending resources related to cycles in nature.

Be sure to let your child know how much you enjoy hearing about what s/he has been learning at school.

Name _____

Directions: Cut out the pictures of the plant at various stages. Sequence the pictures, starting with the seed. Then, glue or tape the pictures in the correct order onto a seperate sheet of paper. Write sentences describing the life cycle of a sunflower on the back of the paper.

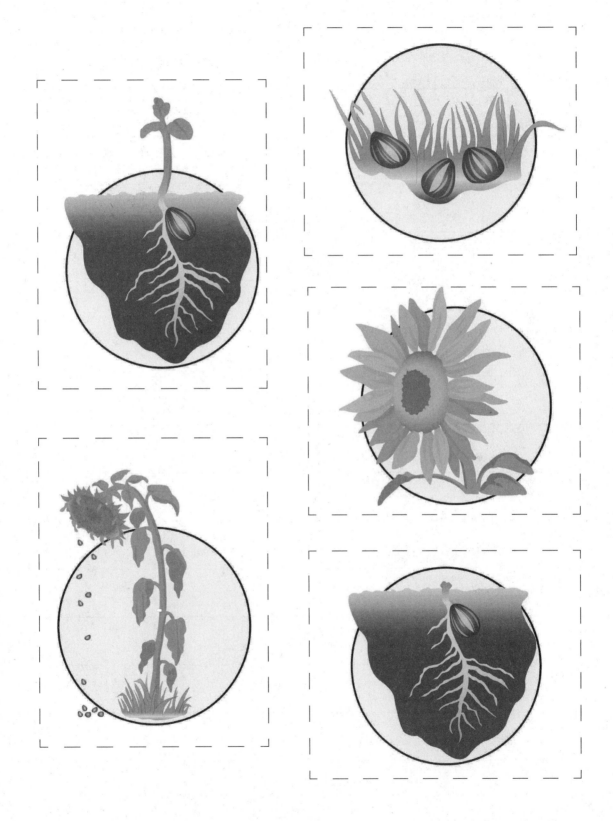

Cycles in Nature

Directions: Write one complete sentence in the first rectangle to introduce your paragraph. Write one complete sentence in the next three rectangles to explain the stages of the life cycle of a frog. Write one complete sentence in the last rectangle to conclude, or finish, your paragraph.

Introductory Sentence:

Explanatory Sentence #1:

Explanatory Sentence #2:

Explanatory Sentence #3:

Concluding Sentence:

Name _____

Directions: Color and cut out the pictures showing the different stages of metamorphosis for a monarch butterfly, and then sequence them in the correct order. Glue or tape the pictures onto drawing paper. Work with a partner to retell the stages of metamorphosis.

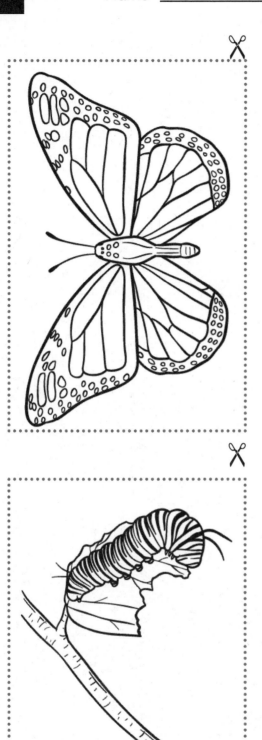

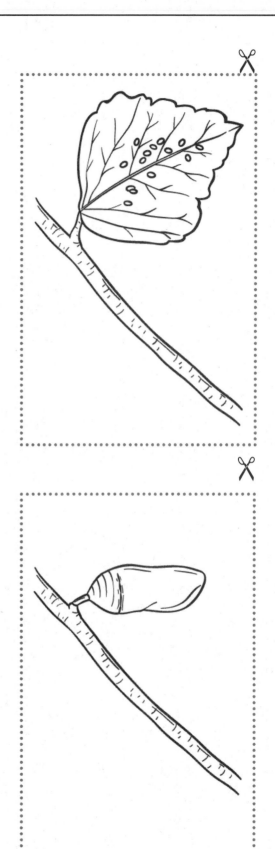

Name _____

Directions: Color and cut out the pictures showing the different stages of metamorphosis for a monarch butterfly, and then sequence them in the correct order. Glue or tape the pictures onto drawing paper. Work with a partner to retell the stages of metamorphosis.

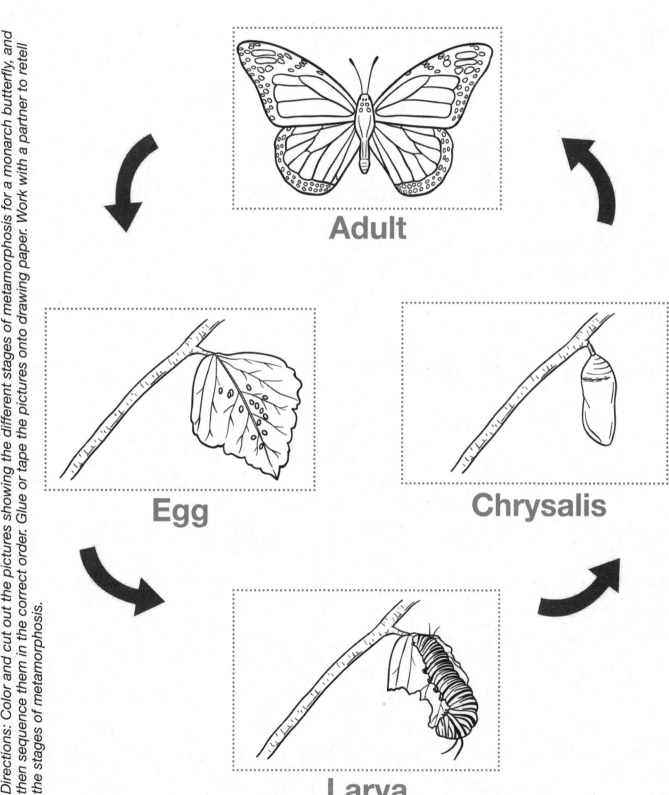

Adult

Egg

Chrysalis

Larva

Name _____

Directions: Listen carefully to the words and sentences read by your teacher. If the sentence uses the word correctly, circle the smiling face. If the sentence does not use the word correctly, circle the frowning face.

1. 🙂 ☹️

2. 🙂 ☹️

3. 🙂 ☹️

4. 🙂 ☹️

5. 🙂 ☹️

6. 🙂 ☹️

7. 🙂 ☹️

8. 🙂 ☹️

9. 🙂 ☹️

10. 🙂 ☹️

Directions: Listen to the sentence read by the teacher. Circle the animal whose life cycle is being described.

1.			
2.			
3.			
4.			
5.			

Name _____

Directions: Listen to the sentence read by the teacher. Circle the smiling face if the sentence is correct. Circle the frowning face if the sentence is not correct.

1.

2.

3.

4.

5.

6.

7.

8.

9.

10.

CORE KNOWLEDGE LANGUAGE ARTS

SERIES EDITOR-IN-CHIEF
E. D. Hirsch, Jr.

PRESIDENT
Linda Bevilacqua

EDITORIAL STAFF
Carolyn Gosse, Senior Editor - Preschool
Khara Turnbull, Materials Development Manager
Michelle L. Warner, Senior Editor - Listening & Learning

Mick Anderson
Robin Blackshire
Maggie Buchanan
Paula Coyner
Sue Fulton
Sara Hunt
Erin Kist
Robin Luecke
Rosie McCormick
Cynthia Peng
Liz Pettit
Ellen Sadler
Deborah Samley
Diane Auger Smith
Sarah Zelinke

DESIGN AND GRAPHICS STAFF
Scott Ritchie, Creative Director

Kim Berrall
Michael Donegan
Liza Greene
Matt Leech
Bridget Moriarty
Lauren Pack

CONSULTING PROJECT MANAGEMENT SERVICES
ScribeConcepts.com

ADDITIONAL CONSULTING SERVICES
Ang Blanchette
Dorrit Green
Carolyn Pinkerton

ACKNOWLEDGMENTS

These materials are the result of the work, advice, and encouragement of numerous individuals over many years. Some of those singled out here already know the depth of our gratitude; others may be surprised to find themselves thanked publicly for help they gave quietly and generously for the sake of the enterprise alone. To helpers named and unnamed we are deeply grateful.

CONTRIBUTORS TO EARLIER VERSIONS OF THESE MATERIALS
Susan B. Albaugh, Kazuko Ashizawa, Nancy Braier, Kathryn M. Cummings, Michelle De Groot, Diana Espinal, Mary E. Forbes, Michael L. Ford, Ted Hirsch, Danielle Knecht, James K. Lee, Diane Henry Leipzig, Martha G. Mack, Liana Mahoney, Isabel McLean, Steve Morrison, Juliane K. Munson, Elizabeth B. Rasmussen, Laura Tortorelli, Rachael L. Shaw, Sivan B. Sherman, Miriam E. Vidaver, Catherine S. Whittington, Jeannette A. Williams

We would like to extend special recognition to Program Directors Matthew Davis and Souzanne Wright who were instrumental to the early development of this program.

SCHOOLS
We are truly grateful to the teachers, students, and administrators of the following schools for their willingness to field test these materials and for their invaluable advice: Capitol View Elementary, Challenge Foundation Academy (IN), Community Academy Public Charter School, Lake Lure Classical Academy, Lepanto Elementary School, New Holland Core Knowledge Academy, Paramount School of Excellence, Pioneer Challenge Foundation Academy, New York City PS 26R (The Carteret School), PS 30X (Wilton School), PS 50X (Clara Barton School), PS 96Q, PS 102X (Joseph O. Loretan), PS 104Q (The Bays Water), PS 214K (Michael Friedsam), PS 223Q (Lyndon B. Johnson School), PS 308K (Clara Cardwell), PS 333Q (Goldie Maple Academy), Sequoyah Elementary School, South Shore Charter Public School, Spartanburg Charter School, Steed Elementary School, Thomas Jefferson Classical Academy, Three Oaks Elementary, West Manor Elementary.

And a special thanks to the CKLA Pilot Coordinators Anita Henderson, Yasmin Lugo-Hernandez, and Susan Smith, whose suggestions and day-to-day support to teachers using these materials in their classrooms was critical.

Credits

Every effort has been taken to trace and acknowledge copyrights. The editors tender their apologies for any accidental infringement where copyright has proved untraceable. They would be pleased to insert the appropriate acknowledgment in any subsequent edition of this publication. Trademarks and trade names are shown in this publication for illustrative purposes only and are the property of their respective owners. The references to trademarks and trade names given herein do not affect their validity.

The Word Work exercises are based on the work of Beck, McKeown, and Kucan in Bringing Words to Life *(The Guilford Press, 2002).*

All photographs are used under license from Shutterstock, Inc. unless otherwise noted.

Expert Reviewer
Margaret S. Saha

Writers
Rosie McCormick

Illustrators and Image Sources
Take-Home Icon: Core Knowledge Staff; 4B-1: Shutterstock; 4B-1 (Answer Key): Shutterstock; PP-1: Shutterstock; DA-2 (butterfly): Shutterstock; DA-2 (frog): Shutterstock; DA-2 (hen): Core Knowledge Staff; DA-2 (butterfly) (Answer Key): Shutterstock; DA-2 (frog) (Answer Key): Shutterstock; DA-2 (hen) (Answer Key): Core Knowledge Staff

Regarding the Shutterstock items listed above, please note: "No person or entity shall falsely represent, expressly or by way of reasonable implication, that the content herein was created by that person or entity, or any person other than the copyright holder(s) of that content."

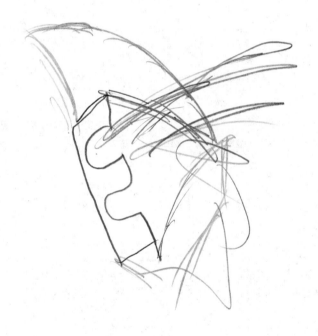